HOUGHTON BOOKS IN LITERATURE

KENNETH S. LYNN · ADVISORY EDITOR

DESIGNS FOR READING

- ○ Plays
- ○ Poems
- ○ Short Stories
- ○ Nonfiction Prose

THE RANGE OF LITERATURE

- ○ Drama
- ● Poetry
- ○ Fiction
- ○ Nonfiction Prose

HOUGHTON
BOOKS IN
LITERATURE

THE RANGE OF LITERATURE:

Poetry

JOHN A. MYERS, JR.

CAROL MARSHALL

HOUGHTON MIFFLIN COMPANY· BOSTON

NEW YORK ATLANTA GENEVA, ILLINOIS DALLAS PALO ALTO

ABOUT THE AUTHORS AND EDITOR

John A. Myers, Jr. has written widely about the teaching of poetry and taken an active part in recent programs to improve the teaching of English in the nation's schools. He has taught both composition and literature in summer institutes for teachers, such as the ones at Rutgers University and at Miles College in Birmingham, Alabama. He was also a member of the Commission on English, established by the College Entrance Examination Board. Mr. Myers teaches English at the Belmont Hill School in Massachusetts.

Carol Marshall has taught many subjects, from arithmetic to aesthetics, to many ages. She writes for the professional journals about literature — especially poetry — and art, and about the art of teaching. She is now teaching English at the Katherine Delmar Burke School in San Francisco.

Kenneth S. Lynn, advisory editor for the Houghton Books in Literature, is an authority in American literature. The author of *Mark Twain and Southwestern Humor* and *The Dream of Success: A Study of the Modern American Imagination,* he is also preëminent for his editing of classic American writers. Dr. Lynn is now Chairman of American Studies at Federal City College in Washington, D.C.

ACKNOWLEDGMENTS

Grateful acknowledgment is made to publishers, agents, and authors for permission to reprint the following poems:

"Anthem for Doomed Youth," from Wilfred Owen; *Collected Poems* edited by C. Day Lewis. Copyright Chatto & Windus Ltd., 1946, © 1963. Reprinted by permission of New Directions Publishing Corporation and Mr. Harold Owen.

"Apparently with No Surprise," by Emily Dickinson. Reprinted by permission of the publishers and the Trustees of Amherst College from Thomas H. Johnson, Editor, *The Poems of Emily Dickinson,* Cambridge, Mass.: The Belknap Press of Harvard University Press, Copyright, 1951, 1955, by the President and Fellows of Harvard College.

"Arms and the Boy," from Wilfred Owen; *Collected Poems* edited by C. Day Lewis. Copyright Chatto & Windus Ltd., 1946, © 1963. Reprinted by permission of New Directions Publishing Corporation and Mr. Harold Owen.

"As the spring rains fall," by Buson from *An Introduction to Haiku* by Harold G. Henderson. Copyright © 1958 by Harold G. Henderson. Reprinted by permission of Doubleday & Company, Inc.

"Auto Wreck," by Karl Shapiro. Copyright 1941 by Karl Shapiro. Reprinted from *Selected Poems* by Karl Shapiro, by permission of Random House, Inc.

"Ballad of Fine Days," from *Times Three* by Phyllis McGinley. Copyright 1943 by Phyllis McGinley. Originally appeared in *The New Yorker.* Reprinted by permission of The Viking Press, Inc.

"Bereft," from *Complete Poems of Robert Frost.* Copyright 1916, 1923, 1928, 1930, 1939 by Holt, Rinehart and Winston, Inc. Copyright 1936, 1942, 1944, 1951, © 1956 by Robert Frost. Copyright © 1964, 1967 by Lesley Frost Ballantine. Reprinted by permission of Holt, Rinehart and Winston, Inc.

"The Bloody Sire," by Robinson Jeffers. Copyright 1941 by Robinson Jeffers. Reprinted from *Selected Poems* by Robinson Jeffers, by permission of Random House, Inc.

"Blooms on the plum," by Rosen from *An Introduction to Haiku* by Harold G. Henderson. Copyright © 1958 by Harold G. Henderson. Reprinted by permission of Doubleday & Company, Inc.

"The Boarder," by Louis Simpson. Copyright © 1959 by Louis Simpson. Reprinted from *A Dream of Governors* by Louis Simpson, by permission of Wesleyan University Press.

"Boy at the Window," by Richard Wilbur. Copyright, 1952 by The New Yorker Magazine, Inc. Reprinted from *Things of This World* by Richard Wilbur by permission of Harcourt, Brace & World, Inc.

"Bredon Hill," by A. E. Housman from "A Shropshire Lad" — Authorized Edition — from *The Collected Poems of A. E. Housman.* Copyright 1939, 1940, © 1959 by Holt, Rinehart and Winston, Inc. Copyright © 1967, 1968 by Robert E. Symons. Reprinted by permission of Holt, Rinehart and Winston, Inc., The Society of Authors as literary representatives of the Estate of A. E. Housman, and Messrs. Jonathan Cape Ltd., publishers *Collected Poems.*

"Channel Firing," from *Collected Poems* by Thomas Hardy, by permission of his Estate; Macmillan & Co. Ltd., London; and The Macmillan Company of Canada Limited.

"The City of Yes and the City of No," from *Bratsk Station and Other New Poems* by Yevgeny Yevtushenko. Copyright 1966 by Sun Books Pty Ltd. Reprinted by permission of Doubleday & Company, Inc.

"Cliff Klingenhagen," by Edwin Arlington Robinson. Reprinted with permission of Charles Scribner's Sons from *The Children of the Night* by Edwin Arlington Robinson (1897).

"Clouds come from time to time," by Basho from *An Introduction to Haiku* by Harold G. Henderson. Copyright © 1958 by Harold G. Henderson. Reprinted by permission of Doubleday & Company, Inc.

"The Conquerors," from *Times Three* by Phyllis McGinley. Copyright © 1958 by Phyllis McGinley. Reprinted by permission of The Viking Press, Inc.

"Conversation with Grandfather," by Charles Arnhold. Reprinted by permission from *Literary Cavalcade,* © 1962 by Scholastic Magazines, Inc.

"Departmental," from *Complete Poems of Robert Frost.* Copyright 1916, 1923, 1928, 1930, 1939 by Holt, Rinehart and Winston, Inc. Copyright 1936, 1942, 1944, 1951, © 1956 by Robert Frost. Copyright © 1964, 1967 by Lesley Frost Ballantine. Reprinted by permission of Holt, Rinehart and Winston, Inc.

"Dinner Guest: Me," by Langston Hughes. From *The Panther and the Lash* by Langston Hughes. © Copyright 1967 by Langston Hughes. Reprinted by permission of Alfred A. Knopf, Inc.

"Dulce Et Decorum Est," from *Wilfred Owen; Collected Poems* edited by C. Day Lewis. Copyright Chatto & Windus Ltd., 1946, © 1963. Reprinted by permission of New Directions Publishing Corporation and Mr. Harold Owen.

"Dust of Snow," from *Complete Poems of Robert Frost.* Copyright 1916, 1923, 1928, 1930, 1939 by Holt, Rinehart and Winston, Inc. Copyright 1936, 1942, 1944, 1951, © 1956 by Robert Frost. Copyright © 1964, 1967 by Lesley Frost Ballantine. Reprinted by permission of Holt, Rinehart and Winston, Inc.

"The Eagle and the Mole," by Elinor Wylie. Copyright 1921 and renewed 1949 by William Rose Benét. Reprinted from *Collected Poems of Elinor Wylie,* by permission of Alfred A. Knopf, Inc.

"Eight O'Clock," from *The Collected Poems of A. E. Housman.* Copyright 1922 by Holt, Rinehart and Winston, Inc. Copyright 1950 by Barclays Bank Ltd. Reprinted by permission of Holt, Rinehart and Winston, Inc., The Society of Authors as literary representatives of the Estate of A. E. Housman, and Messrs. Jonathan Cape Ltd., publishers *Collected Poems.*

"Miniver Cheevy," (copyright 1907 Charles Scribner's Sons; renewal copyright 1935) is reprinted with the permission of Charles Scribner's Sons from *The Town Down the River* by Edwin Arlington Robinson (1897).

"My Papa's Waltz," copyright 1942 by Hearst Magazines, Inc., from *The Collected Poems of Theodore Roethke*. Reprinted by permission of Doubleday & Company, Inc.

"Negro Hero," from *Selected Poems* by Gwendolyn Brooks. Copyright 1945 by Gwendolyn Brooks Blakely. Reprinted by permission of Harper & Row, Publishers.

"The Net," by Sara Teasdale. Reprinted with permission of the Macmillan Company from *Collected Poems* by Sara Teasdale. Copyright 1920 by The Macmillan Company, renewed 1948 by Mamie T. Wheless.

"Nothing Gold Can Stay," from *Complete Poems of Robert Frost*. Copyright 1916, 1923, 1928, 1930, 1939 by Holt, Rinehart and Winston, Inc. Copyright 1936, 1942, 1944, 1951, © 1956 by Robert Frost. Copyright © 1964, 1967 by Lesley Frost Ballantine. Reprinted by permission of Holt, Rinehart and Winston, Inc.

"Out, Out," from *Complete Poems of Robert Frost*. Copyright 1916, 1923, 1928, 1930, 1939 by Holt, Rinehart and Winston, Inc. Copyright 1936, 1942, 1944, 1951, © 1956 by Robert Frost. Copyright © 1964, 1967 by Lesley Frost Ballantine. Reprinted by permission of Holt, Rinehart and Winston, Inc.

"The Parable of the Old Man and the Young," from Wilfred Owen; *Collected Poems* edited by C. Day Lewis. Copyright Chatto & Windus Ltd., 1946, © 1963. Reprinted by permission of New Directions Publishing Corporation and Mr. Harold Owen.

"Pastoral," by Robert Hillyer. From *Collected Poems* by Robert Hillyer. Copyright 1933 and renewed 1961 by Robert Hillyer. Reprinted by permission of Alfred A. Knopf, Inc.

"Patterns," by Paul Simon. Copyright © 1965 Charing Cross Music. Used with permission of the Publisher.

"Pied Beauty," by Gerard Manley Hopkins from *Poems of Gerard Manley Hopkins*, Third Edition edited by W. H. Gardner. Copyright 1948 by Oxford University Press, Inc.

"Poor Timing," copyright, 1940, by Phyllis McGinley. Copyright renewed, 1968, by Phyllis McGinley. From *A Pocketful of Wry* by Phyllis McGinley, by permission of Duell, Sloan and Pearce, affiliate of Meredith Press.

"Portrait of the Artist as a Prematurely Old Man," by Ogden Nash from *Verses from 1929 On*. Copyright, 1934, by The Curtis Publishing Company.

"Prelude I," from *Collected Poems* 1901–1962 by T. S. Eliot, copyright, 1936, by Harcourt, Brace & World, Inc., copyright © 1963, 1964 by T. S. Eliot. Reprinted by permission of the publishers and Faber and Faber Ltd.

"Presentiment" by Emily Dickinson. Reprinted by permission of the publishers and the Trustees of Amherst College from Thomas H. Johnson, Editor, *The Poems of Emily Dickinson*, Cambridge, Mass.: The Belknap Press of Harvard

University Press, Copyright, 1951, 1955, by the President and Fellows of Harvard College.

"Richard Cory," reprinted with permission of Charles Scribner's Sons from *The Children of the Night* by Edwin Arlington Robinson (1897).

"The Savage Beast," from William Carlos Williams, *Collected Later Poems.* Copyright 1948 by William Carlos Williams. Reprinted by permission of New Directions Publishing Corporation.

"Seaside Golf," by John Betjeman from *Collected Poems.* Reprinted by permission of John Murray Ltd.

"A Semi-Revolution," from *Complete Poems of Robert Frost.* Copyright 1916, 1923, 1928, 1930, 1939 by Holt, Rinehart and Winston, Inc. Copyright 1936, 1942, 1944, 1951, © 1956 by Robert Frost. Copyright © 1964, 1967 by Lesley Frost Ballantine. Reprinted by permission of Holt, Rinehart and Winston, Inc.

"Silence," by Marianne Moore. Reprinted with permission of The Macmillan Company from *Collected Poems* by Marianne Moore. Copyright 1935 by Marianne Moore, renewed 1963 by Marianne Moore and T. S. Eliot.

"Sonnet to My Mother," by George Barker from *Collected Poems* 1930 to 1965 by George Granville Barker. Reprinted by permission of October House, Inc. and Faber and Faber Ltd.

"Spring," by Gerard Manley Hopkins from *Poems of Gerard Manley Hopkins,* Third Edition edited by W. H. Gardner. Copyright 1948 by Oxford University Press, Inc.

"Spring and All," William Carlos Williams, *Collected Earlier Poems.* Copyright 1938 by William Carlos Williams. Reprinted by permission of New Directions Publishing Corporation.

"Stopping by Woods on a Snowy Evening," from *Complete Poems of Robert Frost.* Copyright 1916, 1923, 1928, 1930, 1939 by Holt, Rinehart and Winston, Inc. Copyright 1936, 1942, 1944, 1951, © 1956 by Robert Frost. Copyright © 1964, 1967 by Lesley Frost Ballantine. Reprinted by permission of Holt, Rinehart and Winston, Inc.

"Target," by R. P. Lister. Copyright © 1959, The New Yorker Magazine, Inc. Reprinted by permission of Ashley Famous Agency, Inc.

"Terrence, This Is Stupid Stuff," from "A Shropshire Lad" — Authorized Edition — from *The Collected Poems of A. E. Housman.* Copyright 1939, 1940, © 1959 by Holt, Rinehart and Winston, Inc. Copyright © 1967, 1968 by Robert E. Symons. Reprinted by permission of Holt, Rinehart and Winston, Inc. and The Society of Authors as literary representatives of the Estate of A. E. Housman, and Messrs. Jonathan Cape Ltd., publishers *Collected Poems.*

"To an American Poet Just Dead," from *Ceremony and Other Poems,* copyright 1948, 1949, 1950 by Richard Wilbur. Reprinted by permission of Harcourt, Brace & World, Inc.

"To cherry blooms I come," by Buson from *An Introduction to Haiku* by Harold G. Henderson. Copyright © 1958 by Harold G. Henderson. Reprinted by permission of Doubleday & Company, Inc.

"A Total Revolution — An Answer for Robert Frost," by Oscar Williams from *A Little Treasury of Modern Poetry* (New York 1946, 1950) by permission of the Executors of the Estate of Oscar Williams.

"The Turtle," by Ogden Nash. Copyright 1940 by Ogden Nash. Reprinted from *Verses from 1929 On* by permission of Little, Brown and Company, Inc.

"Two Jazz Poems," by Carl Wendell Hines, Jr. from *American Negro Poetry*. Reprinted by permission of the author.

"The Umpire," by Walker Gibson from *The Reckless Spenders*. Reprinted by permission of Indiana University Press.

"The usually hateful crow," by Basho from *An Introduction to Haiku* by Harold G. Henderson. Copyright © 1958 by Harold G. Henderson. Reprinted by permission of Doubleday & Company, Inc.

"We Real Cool," from *Selected Poems* by Gwendolyn Brooks. Copyright 1959 by Gwendolyn Brooks Blakely. Reprinted by permission of Harper & Row, Publishers.

"what if a much of a which of a wind," copyright, 1944, by E. E. Cummings. Reprinted from his volume POEMS 1923–1954, by permission of Harcourt, Brace & World, Inc.

"when serpents bargain for the right to squirm," copyright, 1950, by E. E. Cummings. Reprinted from his volume POEMS 1923–1954, by permission of Harcourt, Brace & World, Inc.

"Without Benefit of Declaration," by Langston Hughes. From *The Panther and the Lash* by Langston Hughes. © Copyright 1967 by Langston Hughes. Reprinted by permission of Alfred A. Knopf, Inc.

CONTENTS

The Poem: from Statement to Detail

The Poem: from Subject to Theme

The Language of a Poem

The Poem and Its Speaker

Rhythm, Sound, and Syntax

Poems for Pleasure

Poetry

1

The Poem:
from Statement to Detail

Poems often seem worlds apart from the prose we read: they look different, they *feel* different as we read them. In some important ways, poems *are* different from prose, whether the prose is fiction or nonfiction. For one thing, poems are more formal, more carefully shaped and arranged on the page. Almost everybody notices, for instance, that certain words in the poem often rhyme and that this rhyming often has a pattern, a regularity. The reader may also sense that the poem has a kind of rhythm or beat that is repeated in successive lines. And in reading the poem he may experience a strange pleasure, an appeal to something beyond mere reason.

But few readers can manage a poem as easily as they can a paragraph of prose. Usually they fail to see the connection between the general statements the poem makes and the concrete details in the poem — the pictures it paints, the images it evokes. The poem may seem a mere random collection of details without any coherent meaning.

The differences between poetry and prose are important, and later we shall see how the special characteristics of poetry contribute to a poem's overall "meaning" and help to give the poem power. This chapter, however, rather than dwelling on the *differences* between poetry and prose, will consider some fundamental ways in which they are alike. By this means we may hope to discover a reliable and familiar way of arriving at a poem's meaning.

Begin with the recognition that a poem and a piece of prose are both built on the same underlying principle: there is always an important relationship between the general statements and the particular details. In any kind of writing there is always this back-and-forth movement between the general and the particular. It might even be said that the general statements "generate" the details which are needed to exemplify or give body to the general idea. This principle can be seen in a few lines from Shakespeare:

> Sweet are the uses of adversity,
> Which like the toad, ugly and venomous,
> Wears yet a precious jewel in his head. . . .

Here the first line states a proposition in general terms. How does the description of the legendary toad exemplify this general idea? (Do the second and third lines also *clarify* the idea of the first line? How?)

The principle underlying these lines of poetry also holds true of a paragraph of prose, an entire essay, or a short story. In a paragraph we speak of the "topic sentence," which expresses the general idea of the paragraph — recognizing that the other sentences provide the facts, details, and examples which develop this idea and give it concrete substance. Sometimes the general statements may be *implied* rather than stated, but the details in the piece are no less controlled by the topic idea for that reason. They are still related to each other *because* they are somehow embodiments of a general idea or observation, either stated or implied. In a short story, we know that such things as plot, character development, and descriptive details are the ingredients in terms of which the *theme* or general idea is realized: alert reading consists of recognizing the relationship among these ingredients that will provide the clue to the story's meaning. This principle seems obvious in connection with the structure of a paragraph or a short story, but it is often overlooked in the reading of a poem.

1. The Poem as Story

Let us now turn to some poems that are like stories and see if we can discover how the details relate to some general idea, stated or implied, to give us the poem's meaning. In reading a story poem, the first thing to do is grasp the basic situation, the *plot* of the poem, so to speak, and the characters involved in this plot. Relating these elements to the more concrete details of language may then reveal how all these things work together to give the poem its meaning.

THE THREE RAVENS

Anonymous

There were three ravens sat on a tree,
  Downe a downe, hay downe, hay downe.
There were three ravens sat on a tree,
  With a downe.
There were three ravens sat on a tree, 5
They were as blacke as they might be.
  With a downe derrie, derrie, derrie,
    downe, downe.

The one of them said to his mate,
"Where shall we our breakfast take?"

"Downe in yonder greene field, 10
There lies a knight slain under his shield.

"His hounds they lie downe at his feete,
So well they can their master keepe.

"His haukes they flie so eagerly,
There's no fowle dare him come nie." 15

Downe there comes a fallow doe,
As great with yong as she might goe.

She lift up his bloudy hed,
And kist his wounds that were so red.

She got him up upon her backe, 20
And carried him to earthen lake.*

21. *lake:* pit.

She buried him before the prime,*
She was dead herself ere evensong time.

God send every gentleman
Such haukes, such hounds, and such a leman.*   25

22. *prime:* 6 a.m.   25. *leman:* beloved lady, sweetheart.

THE TWA CORBIES*

Anonymous

As I was walking all alane,
I heard twa corbies making a mane*;
The tane* unto the t'other say,
"Where sall we gang* and dine today?"

"In behint yon auld fail dyke,*   5
I wot there lies a new-slain knight;
And naebody kens* that he lies there,
But his hawk, his hound, and lady fair.

"His hound is to the hunting gane,
His hawk to fetch the wild-fowl hame,   10
His lady's ta'en another mate,
So we may mak our dinner sweet.

"Ye'll sit on his white hause-bane,*
And I'll pike out his bonny blue een*;
With ae* lock o his gowden hair   15
We'll theek* our nest when it grows bare.

"Mony a one for him makes mane,
But nane sall ken where he is gane;
O'er his white banes, when they are bare,
The wind sall blaw for evermair."   20

* The Two Ravens.   2. *mane:* moan.   3. *tane:* one.   4. *gang:* go.   5. *auld
fail dyke:* old turf wall.   7. *kens:* knows.   13. *hause-bane:* neckbone.
14. *een:* eyes.   15. *ae:* a.   16. *theek:* thatch.

Questions and Exercises

1. Explain what happens and what has already happened in "The Three Ravens." There are seven "characters" in this poem (if "hounds" and "haukes" are regarded as two characters). Be sure to mention the role of each character.

2. The last two lines express a *general* idea or sentiment. You can relate this general idea to the details of the poem by answering the following questions.
   a. What activity is being performed by the hounds and the hawks? What important human virtue is represented by their activity?
   b. Who is the "fallow doe" in line 16? What do her actions have in common with those of the hounds and hawks? What condition is she in? What causes her death? What is the significance of her being "great with yong"? Is her action in some sense climactic? What does the poet gain by calling her a "fallow doe"?

3. What is the basic difference in attitude and behavior between the three ravens, on the one hand, and the hounds, hawks, and doe on the other? How is this difference dramatized in the poem? How does this basic difference between the two groups point up the underlying theme of the poem?

4. "The Twa Corbies" contains no general statements, only dialogue and descriptive details. By carefully examining the details as you did with "The Three Ravens," see if you can determine what kind of "statement" this poem makes. In how many ways is this poem, so similar in some respects to "The Three Ravens," exactly the opposite in its meaning and effect and in the general attitude toward life which it expresses?

5. Write an essay comparing and contrasting the two poems.

EDWARD

Anonymous

"Why dois* your brand* sae drap wi bluid,
    Edward, Edward,
Why dois your brand sae drap wi bluid,
    And why sae sad gang* yee O?"
"O I hae killed my hauke sae guid,   ⁵
    Mither, mither,

1. *dois:* does. *brand:* sword.   4. *gang:* go.

O I hae killed my hauke sae guid,
  And I had nae mair bot hee O."

"Your haukis bluid was nevir sae reid,
        Edward, Edward,   10
Your haukis bluid was nevir sae reid,
  My deir son I tell thee O."
"O I hae killed my reid-roan steid,
        Mither, mither,
O I hae killed my reid-roan steid,   15
  That erst* was sae fair and frie* O."

"Your steid was auld, and ye hae got mair,
        Edward, Edward,
Your steid was auld, and ye hae got mair,
  Sum other dule* ye drie* O."   20
"O I hae killed my fadir deir,
        Mither, mither,
O I hae killed my fadir deir,
  Alas, and wae is mee O!"

"And whatten penance wul ye drie for that,   25
        Edward, Edward,
And whatten penance wul ye drie for that?
  My deir son, now tell me O."
"Ile set my feit in yonder boat,
        Mither, mither,   30
Ile set my feit in yonder boat,
  And Ile fare ovir the sea O."

"And what wul ye doe wi your towirs and your ha,*
        Edward, Edward,
And what wul ye doe wi your towirs and your ha,   35
  That were sae fair to see O?"
"Ile let thame stand tul they doun fa,*

16. *erst:* formerly. *frie:* spirited.   20. *dule:* grief. *drie:* suffer.
33. *ha:* hall.   37. *fa:* fall.

Mither, mither,
Ile let thame stand tul they doun fa,
  For here nevir mair maun* I bee O." 40

"And what wul ye leive to your bairns* and your wife,
    Edward, Edward,
And what wul ye leive to your bairns and your wife,
  Whan ye gang ovir the sea O?"
"The warldis* room, late them beg thrae* life, 45
    Mither, mither,
The warldis room, late them beg thrae life,
  For thame nevir mair wul I see O."

"And what wul ye leive to your ain mither deir,
    Edward, Edward? 50
And what wul ye leive to your ain mither deir?
  My deir son, now tell me O."
"The curse of hell frae me sall ye beir,
    Mither, mither,
The curse of hell frae me sall ye beir, 55
  Sic* counseils ye gave to me O."

40. *maun:* must.　　　41. *bairns:* children.　　　45. *warldis:* world's.
thrae: through.　　56. *sic:* such.

THE WIFE OF USHER'S WELL
Anonymous

There lived a wife at Usher's Well,
  And a wealthy wife was she;
She had three stout and stalwart sons,
  And sent them o'er the sea.

They hadna been a week from her, 5
  A week but barely ane,*

6. *ane:* one.

Whan word came to the carline* wife
 That her three sons were gane.

They hadna been a week from her,
 A week but barely three,   10
Whan word came to the carline wife
 That her sons she'd never see.

"I wish the wind may never cease,
 Nor fashes* in the flood,
Till my three sons come hame to me, 15
 In earthly flesh and blood."

It fell about the Martinmas,*
 When nights are lang and mirk,*
The carline wife's three sons came home,
 And their hats were o the birk.*   20

It neither grew in syke* nor ditch,
 Nor yet in ony sheugh*;
But at the gates o' Paradise,
 That birk grew fair eneugh.

"Blow up the fire, my maidens,   25
 Bring water from the well;
For a' my house shall feast this night,
 Since my three sons are well."

And she has made to them a bed,
 She's made it large and wide,   30
And she's taen her mantle her about,
 Sat down at the bed-side.

Up then crew the red, red cock,
 And up and crew the gray;

7. *carline:* peasant. 14. *fashes:* troubles. 17. *Martinmas:* feast of St.
Martin, November 11. 18. *mirk:* dark. 20. *birk:* birch.
21. *syke:* trench. 22. *ony sheugh:* any furrow.

The eldest to the youngest said,   35
  "'Tis time we were away."

The cock he hadna crawd but once,
  And clappd his wings at a',
When the youngest to the eldest said,
  "Brother we must awa.   40

"The cock doth craw, the day doth daw,
  The channerin* worm doth chide;
Gin* we be mist out o our place,
  A sair pain we maun bide.*

"Fare ye weel, my mother dear!   45
  Fareweel to barn and byre!
And fare ye weel, the bonny lass
  That kindles my mother's fire!"

42. *channerin:* grumbling.   43. *Gin:* if.   44. *maun bide:* must endure.

Questions and Exercises

1. Reconstruct in your own words the story of "Edward." Which details in the poem add to our growing realization of what has happened? Which gradually reveal Edward's state of mind?

2. What has been the mother's role in the story? Explain the probable relationship between the mother and Edward, the mother and the father. Account for Edward's outburst at the end.

3. Is any idea or comment implied by the events of this poem?

4. Tell the story implied in "The Wife of Usher's Well."

5. Point out details in the poem that suggest the mother's excitement and joy. (Notice that we are not *told* in so many words that the mother is excited and joyful; her feelings are *dramatized*.)

6. Although the crowing of the cock is a natural feature of farm life, it has a special significance in this situation. What is it? How is the cock's crowing connected with "the channerin worm"?

7. What is implied by having the youngest son say farewell to "the bonny lass"? How does this intensify the pathos of the sons' situation? What special effect comes from the fact that the bonny lass "kindles my mother's fire"? State the "meaning" of this poem in your own words.

OUT, OUT

Robert Frost

(1874–1963)

The buzz-saw snarled and rattled in the yard
And made dust and dropped stove-length sticks
    of wood,
Sweet-scented stuff when the breeze drew across it.
And from there those that lifted eyes could count
Five mountain ranges one behind the other   5
Under the sunset far into Vermont.
And the saw snarled and rattled, snarled and rattled,
As it ran light, or had to bear a load.
And nothing happened: day was all but done.
Call it a day, I wish they might have said   10
To please the boy by giving him the half hour
That a boy counts so much when saved from work.
His sister stood beside them in her apron
To tell them "Supper." At the word, the saw,
As if to prove saws knew what supper meant,   15
Leaped out at the boy's hand, or seemed to leap —
He must have given the hand. However it was,
Neither refused the meeting. But the hand!
The boy's first outcry was a rueful laugh,
As he swung toward them holding up the hand   20
Half in appeal, but half as if to keep
The life from spilling. Then the boy saw all —
Since he was old enough to know, big boy
Doing a man's work, though a child at heart —
He saw all spoiled. "Don't let them cut my hand   25
    off —
The doctor, when he comes. Don't let him, sister!"
So. But the hand was gone already.
The doctor put him in the dark of ether.
He lay and puffed his lips out with his breath.
And then — the watcher at his pulse took fright.   30

No one believed. They listened at his heart.
Little — less — nothing! — and that ended it.
No more to build on there. And they, since they
Were not the one dead, turned to their affairs.

Questions and Exercises

This poem dramatizes a single incident in the life of a young boy and the people closest to him. All of the details in the poem are meant to contribute to the reader's sense of the tragedy.

1. The title refers to a speech in Shakespeare's *Macbeth* in which the protagonist, bitterly disillusioned and tormented by life, cries "Out, out, brief candle, Life's but a walking shadow, a poor player, that struts and frets his hour upon the stage, and then is heard no more. It is a tale told by an idiot, full of sound and fury, signifying nothing." What is the relevance of the quotation (and thus the title) to the situation dramatized in the poem? Is the title ironic?

2. How is the buzz-saw portrayed in the poem? Is it made to seem more than an inanimate machine? Why?

3. Find details that reveal the boy's first, second, and third reaction to the accident. What is gained by this progression?

4. By what indirect means does the poet describe the boy's actual death? Is this more effective than simply saying "Then the boy died"? Why?

5. What is the effect of the ending of the poem, with the onlookers turning "to their affairs"? Are they meant to seem callous, or is there some other explanation of their behavior?

Patterns

Amy Lowell

(1874–1925)

I walk down the patterned garden paths
In my stiff, brocaded gown.
With my powdered hair and jeweled fan,
I too am a rare
Pattern. As I wander down   5

The garden paths.
My dress is richly figured,
And the train
Makes a pink and silver stain
On the gravel, and the thrift   10
Of the borders.
Just a plate of current fashion,
Tripping by in high-heeled, ribboned shoes.
Not a softness anywhere about me,
Only whalebone and brocade.   15
And I sink on a seat in the shade
Of a lime tree. For my passion
Wars against the stiff brocade.
The daffodils and squills*
Flutter in the breeze   20
As they please.
And I weep;
For the lime tree is in blossom
And one small flower has dropped upon my bosom.

And the plashing of waterdrops   25
In the marble fountain
Comes down the garden paths.
The dripping never stops.
Underneath my stiffened gown
Is the softness of a woman bathing in a marble   30
    basin,
A basin in the midst of hedges grown
So thick, she cannot see her lover hiding.
But she guesses he is near,
And the sliding of the water
Seems the stroking of a dear   35
Hand upon her.
What is Summer in a fine brocaded gown!
I should like to see it lying in a heap upon the ground.
All the pink and silver crumpled upon the ground.

19. *squills:* The squill is an herb of the lily family.

I would be the pink and silver as I ran along the
    paths,   40
And he would stumble after,
Bewildered by my laughter.
I should see the sun flashing from his sword hilt and
    the buckles on his shoes.
I would choose
To lead him in a maze along the patterned paths,   45
A bright and laughing maze for my heavy-booted
    lover,
Till he caught me in the shade,
And the buttons of his waistcoat bruised my body as
    he clasped me,
Aching, melting, unafraid.
With the shadows of the leaves and the sundrops,   50
And the plopping of the waterdrops,
All about us in the open afternoon —
I am very like to swoon
With the weight of this brocade,
For the sun shifts through the shade.   55

Underneath the fallen blossom
In my bosom
Is a letter I have hid.
It was brought to me this morning by a rider from
    the Duke.
"Madam, we regret to inform you that Lord Hartwell   60
Died in action Thursday se'nnight."
As I read it in the white, morning sunlight,
The letters squirmed like snakes.
"Any answer, Madam," said my footman.
"No," I told him.   65
"See that the messenger takes some refreshment.
No, no answer,"
And I walked into the garden,
Up and down the patterned paths,
In my stiff, correct brocade.   70

The blue and yellow flowers stood up proudly in the sun,
Each one.
I stood upright too,
Held rigid to the pattern
By the stiffness of my gown;   75
Up and down I walked,
Up and down.

In a month he would have been my husband.
In a month, here, underneath this lime,
We would have broke the pattern;   80
He for me, and I for him,
He as Colonel, I as Lady,
On this shady seat.
He had a whim
That sunlight carried blessing.   85
And I answered, "It shall be as you have said."
Now he is dead.
In Summer and in Winter I shall walk
Up and down
The patterned garden paths   90
In my stiff, brocaded gown.
The squills and daffodils
Will give place to pillared roses, and to asters, and to
    snow,
I shall go
Up and down   95
In my gown.
Gorgeously arrayed,
Boned and stayed.
And the softness of my body will be guarded from
    embrace
By each button, hook, and lace.   100
For the man who should loose me is dead,
Fighting with the Duke in Flanders,
In a pattern called a war.
Christ! What are patterns for?

PATTERNS

Paul Simon

(1942–   )

The night set softly
With the hush of falling leaves
Casting shivering shadows
On the houses through the trees

And the light from a street lamp   5
Paints a pattern on my wall
Like the pieces of a puzzle
Or a child's uneven scrawl.

Up a narrow flight of stairs
In a narrow little room   10
As I lie upon my bed
In the early evening gloom

Impaled on my wall
My eyes can dimly see
The pattern of my life   15
And the puzzle that is me.

From the moment of my birth
To the instant of my death
There are patterns I must follow
Just as I must breathe each breath.   20

Like a rat in a maze
The path before me lies
And the pattern never alters
Until the rat dies.

And the pattern still remains   25
On the wall where darkness fell

And it's fitting that it should
For in darkness I must dwell.

Like the color of my skin
Or the day that I grow old   30
My life is made of patterns
That can scarcely be controlled.

Questions and Exercises

Amy Lowell's "Patterns" tells a story of a woman whose life is controlled by patterns of various kinds and whose one chance for freedom and happiness is destroyed by another pattern. The poet dramatizes the tragedy of the woman's life by letting her reveal, as she walks through her formal garden, the thoughts and feelings produced in her by a letter she has received that morning bearing tragic news.

1. The last line of the poem asks a question and in so doing makes a commentary on life. This question (with its implied commentary), together with the title of the poem, constitute a general statement of the poem's theme. What is this theme?

2. The theme of the poem is carefully reflected in its details, in all the patterns that imprison the woman. There are at least fifteen patterns. How many can you identify?

3. Set against the patterns are an almost equal number of items that might be called anti-patterns, things that are natural, spontaneous, free. Can you identify these and tell how they contribute to the meaning of the poem?

4. Assuming that the war in Flanders referred to is a victory won by the Duke of Marlborough in 1708, can you explain why the eighteenth century provides a particularly appropriate setting for the poem? What were gardens, manners, dress like in the eighteenth century?

5. Fit the details of Simon's "Patterns" to its general statements such as "the pattern never alters/Until the rat dies," and "My life is made of patterns/That can scarcely be controlled."

6. Compare this poem to Amy Lowell's "Patterns." What similarities and what differences do you notice in the types of patterns referred to and the effect of these patterns on the lives of the speakers? Which poem is more specific in its use of the imagery of patterns?

2. *The Lyric Poem as Statement and Detail*

The remaining poems in this chapter, like the last poem, are not ballads or narrative poems. They are short lyric poems which achieve their meaning and effect by means other than story or "plot."

Nevertheless, what these poems say continues to depend on the relationship between the general statements and the particular details, the back-and-forth movement that we spoke of earlier. Notice, as before, how the general statements tend to generate the concrete details which, in turn, illustrate and give substance to the statements. The details also enrich the poem by enlarging the implications of the statements.

THE WORLD IS TOO MUCH WITH US
William Wordsworth

(1770–1850)

The world is too much with us; late and soon,
Getting and spending, we lay waste our powers:
Little we see in Nature that is ours;
We have given our hearts away, a sordid boon!
This sea that bares her bosom to the moon;   5
The winds that will be howling at all hours,
And are up-gathered now like sleeping flowers;
For this, for everything, we are out of tune;
It moves us not. Great God! I'd rather be
A pagan suckled in a creed outworn;   10
So might I, standing on this pleasant lea,
Have glimpses that would make me less forlorn;
Have sight of Proteus rising from the sea;
Or hear old Triton blow his wreathèd horn.

Questions and Exercises

Notice that the first four lines (called a quatrain) of this poem, like the topic sentence in a paragraph, make a very general statement about man's preoccupations with material or worldly things, preoccupations ("getting and spending") which have destroyed his appreciation of nature and somehow diminished his "power." According to Wordsworth, man's greatest asset is his "heart"; and the heart, he would maintain, can be *nourished* only by nature, not by the "getting and spending" that goes on in the cities.

1. How do the next four lines (second quatrain) exemplify the general idea expressed in the first quatrain?

2. What idea about the *natural* relationship between the sea and the moon is implied in line 5? How is this relationship contrasted with man's response to nature (lines 8–9)?

3. In line 10 why does the poet say he would rather be a pagan? Rather than what? How would a pagan's view of, and relationship to, nature differ from that of modern man? Why does the poet use the word "suckled"?

4. Look up the mythological figures Proteus and Triton. With what part of nature are these figures identified? Why would the pagan "have glimpses" of these figures, and why would these glimpses make him "less forlorn"? Less forlorn than who?

It Is Not Growing Like a Tree
Ben Jonson
(1573?–1637)

It is not growing like a tree
In bulk, doth make man better be;
Or standing long an oak, three hundred year,
To fall a log at last, dry, bald, and sere:
   A lily of a day   5
   Is fairer far in May,
Although it fall and die that night —
It was the plant and flower of light.
In small proportions we just beauties see;
And in short measures life may perfect be.   10

Exercise

In this ten-line poem, the first two lines and the last two state a general proposition. Explain how the pictures painted in the intervening six lines exactly match or exemplify this proposition. In so doing, state explicitly how the qualities associated with the oak contrast with those associated with the lily and how this contrast ties together the opening and closing statements.

BEREFT

Robert Frost

(1874–1963)

Where had I heard this wind before
Change like this to a deeper roar?
What would it take my standing there for,
Holding open a restive door,
Looking down hill to a frothy shore?   5
Summer was past and day was past.
Somber clouds in the west were massed.
Out in the porch's sagging floor,
Leaves got up in a coil and hissed,
Blindly struck at my knee and missed.   10
Something sinister in the tone
Told me my secret must be known:
Word I was in the house alone
Somehow must have gotten abroad,
Word I was in my life alone,   15
Word I had no one left but God.

Questions and Exercises

1. The last six lines of this poem build gradually toward a climactic general statement of the idea and the emotion that the poet means to convey. The first ten lines contain descriptions of sights and sounds. What is the relationship between the concrete images (the descriptive details) and the general statements? In answering this question consider the following:
    a. What is the weather like? What is the wind doing? What might have been the previous occasion on which the speaker of the poem had heard the "wind" change to a "deeper roar"?
    b. Why is the speaker doing what he is doing?

    c. What time of year is it? What time of day? What is the emotional effect of this setting in time, particularly the combination of the two times?

    d. How does the description of the floor of the house fit in with the other details?

    e. What are the leaves being compared to? What is your feeling of the man's attitude toward nature and of his sense of nature's attitude toward him? (What is the force of the word *blindly*?) How does the implied relationship between man and nature contribute to the meaning of the general statement at the end?

Notice that it is the descriptive *details* of the poem that give the statement at the end its power, its emotional coloring. Try to imagine the difference in effect if the poem consisted only of the last six lines. To *feel* this difference write a paraphrase of the poem and then compare your *experience* of reading your own paraphrase with your *experience* in reading the poem itself. The difference you feel is the measure of poetry itself, which works upon the *senses* and emotions as well as upon the mind.

Read the following three poems carefully, noting the way in which meaning emerges from detail.

Presentiment — is that long Shadow — on the Lawn —
Indicative that Suns go down —
The Notice to the startled Grass
That Darkness — is about to pass —

Emily Dickinson

(1830–1886)

    It dropped so low — in my Regard —
    I heard it hit the Ground —
    And go to pieces on the Stones
    At the bottom of my Mind —

Yet blamed the Fate that fractured — less
Than I reviled Myself,
For entertaining Plated Wares
Upon my Silver Shelf —

Emily Dickinson

(1830–1886)

PRELUDE I

T. S. Eliot

(1888–1965)

The winter evening settles down
With smell of steaks in passageways.
Six o'clock.
The burnt-out ends of smoky days.
And now a gusty shower wraps   5
The grimy scraps
Of withered leaves about your feet
And newspapers from vacant lots;
The showers beat
On broken blinds and chimney-pots,   10
And at the corner of the street
A lonely cab-horse steams and stamps.
And then the lighting of the lamps.

3. The Poem as Detail

The poems in this final section are made up almost entirely of a series of concrete images or actions, with no general statements to play against the descriptive details. In poems like these the reader must discover for himself the statement *implied* by the details. He must search for a unifying idea or attitude or emotion which holds all the details together, much in the way a magnet will draw iron filings into a pattern. This unifying principle will provide the clue to the statement made by the poem.

Here, however, a reminder may be in order. What we have called the *statement* that a poem makes is not the same thing as a message or a moral. It may be no more than the expression of an attitude or an emotion toward a person or an object or an institution that makes us see it in a new light, that gives it a new reality or perspective for us. In any case, the poem is never simply a statement *about* something; it is a freshly-created *experience* of it. Archibald MacLeish, the American poet, has put this idea succinctly: "A poem should not mean but be."

THE EAGLE

Alfred, Lord Tennyson

(1809–1892)

He clasps the crag with crooked hands;
Close to the sun in lonely lands,
Ringed with the azure world, he stands.

The wrinkled sea beneath him crawls;
He watches from his mountain walls,   5
And like a thunderbolt he falls.

Questions and Exercises

1. What is the effect of referring to the eagle's claws as "crooked hands" and saying "he stands"? To what is the eagle being compared?

2. What qualities of the eagle does the poet stress by such expressions as "Close to the sun," "Ringed with the azure world," "The wrinkled sea beneath him *crawls*," "like a thunderbolt"?

3. Write a paragraph in which you explain the "statement" Tennyson is here making about eagles. How does the poet's "statement" differ from the account a zoologist might have given?

The Eagle and the Mole

Elinor Wylie

(1885–1928)

Avoid the reeking herd,
Shun the polluted flock,
Live like that stoic bird,
The eagle of the rock.

The huddled warmth of crowds   5
Begets and fosters hate;
He keeps, above the clouds,
His cliff inviolate.

When flocks are folded warm,
And herds to shelter run,   10
He sails above the storm,
He stares into the sun.

If in the eagle's track
Your sinews cannot leap,
Avoid the lathered pack,   15
Turn from the steaming sheep.

If you would keep your soul
From the spotted sight or sound,
Live like the velvet mole;
Go burrow underground.   20

And there hold intercourse
With roots of trees and stones,
With rivers at their source,
And disembodied bones.

Questions and Exercises

1. Unlike Tennyson's "The Eagle," this poem makes several explicit statements: "Avoid the reeking herd," "The huddled warmth of crowds/Begets and fosters hate," "If you would keep your soul . . . ," etc. These statements, however, are not exactly literal. Their meaning is developed in terms of what the eagle, the sheep, and the mole *stand for*. The concrete and the general are inseparably mixed. The poem gains its force from the concrete associations carried by the three animals.

    Explain what the eagle, the sheep, and the mole stand for. What is this poem, in its largest sense, finally about?

2. Although the "statement" made by this poem is more complex than that made by Tennyson's poem, it is not necessarily a better poem. It is simply a different kind of poem, with a different intention. To what extent do the two poems express the same theme? Which of the two poems do you find more powerful or effective? Explain.

In the following three poems the general idea is either *stated* (and supported by the details) or *implied* by the details alone. Study the poems and see if you can answer the questions which follow.

Departmental

Robert Frost

(1874–1963)

An ant on the tablecloth
Ran into a dormant moth
Of many times his size.
He showed not the least surprise.
His business wasn't with such.   5
He gave it scarcely a touch,
And was off on his duty run.
Yet if he encountered one
Of the hive's enquiry squad
Whose work is to find out God   10

And the nature of time and space,
He would put him onto the case.
Ants are a curious race;
One crossing with hurried tread
The body of one of their dead   15
Isn't given a moment's arrest —
Seems not even impressed.
But he no doubt reports to any
With whom he crosses antennae,
And they no doubt report   20
To the higher up at court.
Then word goes forth in Formic:
"Death's come to Jerry McCormic,
Our selfless forager Jerry.
Will the special Janizary   25
Whose office it is to bury
The dead of the commissary
Go bring him home to his people.
Lay him in state on a sepal.*
Wrap him for shroud in a petal.   30
Embalm him with ichor* of nettle.
This is the word of your Queen."
And presently on the scene
Appears a solemn mortician;
And taking formal position   35
With feelers calmly atwiddle,
Seizes the dead by the middle,
And heaving him high in air,
Carries him out of there.
No one stands round to stare.   40
It is nobody else's affair.

It couldn't be called ungentle.
But how thoroughly departmental.

29. *sepal:* leaflike part of a flower.   31. *ichor:* fluid from the veins of gods.

THE EXPRESS

Stephen Spender

(1909–   )

After the first powerful plain manifesto
The black statement of pistons, without more fuss
But gliding like a queen, she leaves the station.
Without bowing and with restrained unconcern
She passes the houses which humbly crowd outside,   5
The gasworks and at last the heavy page
Of death, printed by gravestones in the cemetery.
Beyond the town there lies the open country
Where, gathering speed, she acquires mystery,
The luminous self-possession of ships on ocean.   10

It is now she begins to sing — at first quite low
Then loud, and at last with a jazzy madness —
The song of her whistle screaming at curves,
Of deafening tunnels, brakes, innumerable bolts.
And always light, aerial, underneath   15
Goes the elate meter of her wheels.
Steaming through metal landscape on her lines
She plunges new eras of wild happiness

Where speed throws up strange shapes, broad curves
And parallels clean like the steel of guns.   20
At last, further than Edinburgh or Rome,
Beyond the crest of the world, she reaches night
Where only a low streamline brightness
Of phosphorus on the tossing hills is white.
Ah, like a comet through flames she moves entranced   25
Wrapt in her music no bird song, no, nor bough
Breaking with honey buds, shall ever equal.

RICHARD CORY

Edwin Arlington Robinson
(1869–1935)

Whenever Richard Cory went down town,
We people on the pavement looked at him:
He was a gentleman from sole to crown,
Clean favored, and imperially slim.

And he was always quietly arrayed,   5
And he was always human when he talked;
But still he fluttered pulses when he said,
"Good morning," and he glittered when he walked.

And he was rich — yes, richer than a king —
And admirably schooled in every grace: 10
In fine, we thought that he was everything
To make us wish that we were in his place.

So on we worked, and waited for the light,
And went without the meat, and cursed the bread;
And Richard Cory, one calm summer night,   15
Went home and put a bullet through his head.

Questions and Exercises

1. "Departmental" seems to be about the behavior of ants. These ants, however, have been *personified,* given human speech, attitudes, and emotions. Why? Is the poem really about ants? What do the ants and their behavior come to symbolize? To what extent does the poem's meaning depend on the general statement made in the last line?

2. Is "The Express" merely a description of a train, or does the train come to stand for something beyond itself? Can this idea be stated *apart from* the various descriptions of the train, or are the idea and

the train inseparable? What clue to the poem's "meaning" (or the train's symbolic significance) is provided in the last two lines?

3. How is the irony of "Richard Cory" (the discrepancy between "we people's" envy of Richard Cory and his own unhappiness, as implied by his suicide) enhanced by the descriptive details of the first three stanzas? To what is Richard compared (by suggestion) in these stanzas? Does the irony which the poem dramatizes point to a more general idea or observation about life?

2

The Poem:
from Subject to Theme

Contrary to the notions of some people, who imagine that poetry must celebrate moonlight and hummingbirds, a poem may be written on any subject whatever. The subject of a poem is the scene or action or object or person or experience it describes. Thus far you have seen poems ranging in subject from the death of a loved one to the behavior of a colony of ants. The subject matter of poetry is as broad as human experience and observation, and it can include every conceivable human emotion, attitude, or idea. In this chapter you will encounter poems on a wide variety of subjects: mending a stone wall, killing a man in a war, a gas attack in a war, an automobile wreck, a man stopping in his wagon to look at some woods, a boy looking out of the window at a snowman, a lifeguard who has failed to rescue a drowning boy, a crow shaking snow out of a tree.

The subject of a poem, however, is not its *theme*. A poem's theme or "meaning" is the idea or observation about life or the attitude that grows out of the subject matter of the poem, the way the subject is presented or dealt with by the language of the poem. Sometimes, as we have shown, the theme is stated in the poem ("The world is too much with us"); sometimes it is only implied.

In Chapter I we saw that a poem about three crows, a slain knight, and his sweetheart can have as its theme the ennobling quality of human compassion, loyalty, and self-sacrifice. We saw that a poem ostensibly about ants had as its theme a comment

on collectivism or bureaucracy or the tendency of life in modern
society to become compartmentalized or categorized.

Let us now look at some poems with widely different subjects
and see how different the subject of a poem can be from its
theme.

MENDING WALL

Robert Frost

(1874–1963)

Something there is that doesn't love a wall,
That sends the frozen-ground-swell under it,
And spills the upper boulders in the sun;
And makes gaps even two can pass abreast.
The work of hunters is another thing: 5
I have come after them and made repair
Where they have left not one stone on a stone,
But they would have the rabbit out of hiding,
To please the yelping dogs. The gaps I mean,
No one has seen them made or heard them made,   10
But at spring mending-time we find them there.
I let my neighbor know beyond the hill;
And on a day we meet to walk the line
And set the wall between us once again.
We keep the wall between us as we go.   15
To each the boulders that have fallen to each.
And some are loaves and some so nearly balls
We have to use a spell to make them balance:
"Stay where you are until our backs are turned!"
We wear our fingers rough with handling them.   20
Oh, just another kind of outdoor game,
One on a side. It comes to little more:
There where it is we do not need the wall:
He is all pine and I am apple orchard.
My apple trees will never get across   25
And eat the cones under his pines, I tell him.

He only says, "Good fences make good neighbors."
Spring is the mischief in me, and I wonder
If I could put a notion in his head:
"*Why* do they make good neighbors? Isn't it   30
Where there are cows? But here there are no cows.
Before I built a wall I'd ask to know
What I was walling in or walling out,
And to whom I was like to give offense.
Something there is that doesn't love a wall,   35
That wants it down." I could say "Elves" to him,
But it's not elves exactly, and I'd rather
He said it for himself. I see him there
Bringing a stone grasped firmly by the top
In each hand, like an old-stone savage armed.   40
He moves in darkness as it seems to me,
Not of woods only and the shade of trees.
He will not go behind his father's saying,
And he likes having thought of it so well
He says again, "Good fences make good neighbors."   45

Questions and Exercises

The subject of this poem, as its title tells us, is the annual springtime
mending of the stone wall separating the property of two New England
land owners, probably farmers. To discover the poem's *theme* consider
the way the poet handles the details of description and dialogue.

1. Why does the poet use the word *something* in line 1? Defend the
   proposition that we could insert the words *in nature* after "Some-
   thing there is. . . ." Why is this *natural* cause of the wall's destruc-
   tion so carefully distinguished from "the work of hunters"?

2. Why does the speaker call the act of repairing the wall "a kind of
   outdoor *game*"? Why is the wall actually unnecessary?

3. Explain the neighbor's reasons for believing that walls are important.
   From whom did the neighbor get his idea about the importance of
   walls? Would it be fair to call his "good fences make good neigh-
   bors" a cliché? What basic human tendency does the neighbor's
   attitude toward walls represent? How does his attitude contrast
   with that of the speaker?

4. Why is the speaker tempted to say "Elves" to his neighbor? Explain carefully the significance of the phrases "like an old stone savage armed" and "He moves in darkness."

5. What is the theme of this poem?

THE MAN HE KILLED

Thomas Hardy

(1840–1928)

"Had he and I but met
By some old ancient inn,
We should have sat us down to wet
Right many a nipperkin!*

"But ranged as infantry   5
And staring face to face,
I shot at him as he at me,
And killed him in his place.

"I shot him dead because —
Because he was my foe;   10
Just so: my foe of course he was;
That's clear enough; although

"He thought he'd 'list,* perhaps,
Off-hand-like — just as I —
Was out of work, had sold his traps —   15
No other reason why.

"Yes, quaint and curious war is!
You shoot a fellow down
You'd treat, if met where any bar is,
Or help to half-a-crown."*   20

4. *nipperkin:* half-pint (of ale).   13. *'list:* enlist.   20. *half-a-crown:* British coin.

Questions and Exercises

1. Why does the speaker emphasize the difference between meeting a man in an "old ancient inn" (a pub) and coming up against the same man in a war?

2. What is the special force of the word *ranged* in line 5? Does it also suggest the word *arranged*? Who makes the arrangements and does the arranging for a war?

3. For what common reason did the two "foes" join the army? Did they hate each other? Who or what *defined* them as "foes"?

4. In the third stanza the speaker seeks an explanation for killing a man he didn't even know. What devices does the poet use to show that the speaker is *groping* for an explanation and that the only explanation he can find is highly unsatisfactory?

5. The speaker calls war "quaint and curious." What is the effect of these words in this context? Why can't the speaker see the true nature of war and his relation to it? Is there something ritualistic about war?

6. What basic human tendency does war come to represent in this poem? Compare the theme of this poem with that of "Mending Wall." To what extent do these two poems have the same theme?

DULCE ET DECORUM EST

Wilfred Owen

(1893–1918)

Bent double, like old beggars under sacks,
Knock-kneed, coughing like hags, we cursed through
    sludge,
Till on the haunting flares we turned our backs
And towards our distant rest began to trudge.
Men marched asleep. Many had lost their boots   5
But limped on, blood-shod. All went lame; all blind;
Drunk with fatigue; deaf even to the hoots
Of gas shells dropping softly behind.

Gas! Gas! Quick, boys! — An ecstasy of fumbling,
Fitting the clumsy helmets just in time;   10

But someone still was yelling out and stumbling
And flound'ring like a man in fire or lime . . .
Dim, through the misty panes and thick green light,
As under a green sea, I saw him drowning.

In all my dreams, before my helpless sight,   15
He plunges at me, guttering, choking, drowning.

If in some smothering dreams you too could pace
Behind the wagon that we flung him in,
And watch the white eyes writhing in his face,
His hanging face, like a devil's sick of sin;   20
If you could hear, at every jolt, the blood
Come gargling from the froth-corrupted lungs,
Obscene as cancer, bitter as the cud
Of vile, incurable sores on innocent tongues, —
My friend, you would not tell with such high zest   25
To children ardent for some desperate glory,
The old Lie: *Dulce et decorum est*
*Pro patria mori.**

27–28. ***Dulce et decorum est/Pro patria mori:*** It is sweet and becoming to die
for one's country. The quotation is from the Roman poet Horace.

Questions and Exercises

This poem appears to be no more than a vivid description of a gas
attack in World War I. In the last stanza, however, the speaker reveals
his *attitude* toward what he is describing, and the description becomes
a commentary on war. The deep *irony* of Horace's statement emerges
when it is contrasted with what it is actually like to die in a modern war.
Other devices of language reinforce this irony.

1. Who is the "you" referred to in line 17 — Horace only? What is
   gained by this direct address to "you"?

2. Is there a connection between such words as *devil's, sin, froth-
   corrupted, innocent,* and *children*? In how many senses are "chil-
   dren" corrupted by war? Is there a contrast between the "children's"
   tongues and Horace's tongue? Does Horace, in the light of his state-
   ment about dying for one's country, come to represent something
   more than himself?

AUTO WRECK

Karl Shapiro

(1913–   )

Its quick soft silver bell beating, beating,
And down the dark one ruby flare
Pulsing out red light like an artery,
The ambulance at top speed floating down
Past beacons and illuminated clocks   5
Wings in a heavy curve, dips down,
And brakes speed, entering the crowd.
The doors leap open, emptying light;
Stretchers are laid out, the mangled lifted
And stowed into the little hospital.   10
Then the bell, breaking the hush, tolls once,
And the ambulance with its terrible cargo
Rocking, slightly rocking, moves away,
As the doors, an afterthought, are closed.

We are deranged, walking among the cops   15
Who sweep glass and are large and composed.
One is still making notes under the light.
One with a bucket douches ponds of blood
Into the street and gutter.
One hangs lanterns on the wrecks that cling,   20
Empty husks of locusts, to iron poles.

Our throats were tight as tourniquets,
Our feet were bound with splints, but now,
Like convalescents intimate and gauche,
We speak through sickly smiles and warn   25
With the stubborn saw of common sense,
The grim joke and the banal resolution.
The traffic moves around with care,
But we remain, touching a wound
That opens to our richest horror.   30
Already old, the question Who shall die?

Becomes unspoken Who is innocent?
For death in war is done by hands;
Suicide has cause and stillbirth, logic;
And cancer, simple as a flower, blooms.   35
But this invites the occult mind,
Cancels our physics with a sneer,
And spatters all we knew of denouement
Across the expedient and wicked stones.

Questions and Exercises

This poem describes the aftermath of a terrible automobile accident. In so doing, however, it probes the meaning of human existence.

1. Stanza three deals with the reactions of the bystanders, including the speaker of the poem. These bystanders are described in language that suggests they are like sick or wounded people. Pick out the expressions that convey this idea.

2. What is the "richest horror" referred to in line 30? How is it related to the two questions "Who shall die?" and "Who is innocent?" What speculation about life do these questions imply?

3. What is the difference between death by war, suicide, and stillbirth, on the one hand, and death by an automobile accident, on the other?

4. Why does "this" (this what?) "invite the occult mind," "cancel our physics," "spatter all we know of denouement?" If you can see what *physics* and *denouement* have in common and why one would have to go beyond physics to the "occult mind" to answer the questions in the mind of the speaker, you will know what the theme of this poem is.

5. Write a paraphrase of the last stanza.

6. Can you relate the elaborate description of the ambulance with its "terrible cargo" in the first stanza to the theme that is developed in the last stanza?

Terence, This Is Stupid Stuff
A. E. Housman

(1859–1936)

"Terence, this is stupid stuff:
You eat your victuals fast enough;
There can't be much amiss, 'tis clear,

To see the rate you drink your beer.
But oh, good Lord, the verse you make,　　5
It gives a chap the belly-ache.
The cow, the old cow, she is dead;
It sleeps well, the horned head:
We poor lads, 'tis our turn now
To hear such tunes as killed the cow.　　10
Pretty friendship 'tis to rhyme
Your friends to death before their time
Moping melancholy mad:
Come, pipe a tune to dance to, lad."

Why, if 'tis dancing you would be,　　15
There's brisker pipes than poetry.
Say, for what were hop-yards meant,
Or why was Burton built on Trent?
Oh many a peer of England brews
Livelier liquor than the Muse,　　20
And malt does more than Milton can
To justify God's ways to man.
Ale, man, ale's the stuff to drink
For fellows whom it hurts to think:
Look into the pewter pot　　25
To see the world as the world's not.
And faith, 'tis pleasant till 'tis past:
The mischief is that 'twill not last.
Oh I have been to Ludlow fair
And left my necktie God knows where,　　30
And carried halfway home, or near,
Pints and quarts of Ludlow beer:

Then the world seemed none so bad,
And I myself a sterling lad;
And down in lovely muck I've lain,　　35
Happy till I woke again.
Then I saw the morning sky:
Heigho, the tale was all a lie;
The world, it was the old world yet,
I was I, my things were wet,　　40

And nothing now remained to do
But begin the game anew.

   Therefore, since the world has still
Much good, but much less good than ill,
And while the sun and moon endure   45
Luck's a chance, but trouble's sure,
I'd face it as a wise man would,
And train for ill and not for good.
'Tis true, the stuff I bring for sale
Is not so brisk a brew as ale: 50
Out of a stem that scored the hand
I wrung it in a weary land.
But take it: if the smack is sour,
The better for the embittered hour;
It should do good to heart and head   55
When your soul is in my soul's stead;
And I will friend you, if I may,
In the dark and cloudy day.

   There was a king reigned in the East:
There, when kings will sit to feast,   60
They get their fill before they think
With poisoned meat and poisoned drink.
He gathered all that springs to birth
From the many-venomed earth;
First a little, thence to more,   65
He sampled all her killing store;
And easy, smiling, seasoned sound,
Sate the king when healths went round.
They put arsenic in his meat
And stared aghast to watch him eat;   70
They poured strychnine in his cup
And shook to see him drink it up:
They shook, they stared as white's their shirt:
Them it was their poison hurt.
— I tell the tale that I heard told.   75
Mithridates, he died old.

CLIFF KLINGENHAGEN

Edwin Arlington Robinson

(1869–1935)

Cliff Klingenhagen had me in to dine
With him one day; and after soup and meat;
And all the other things there were to eat,
Cliff took two glasses and filled one with wine
And one with wormwood.* Then, without a sign   5
For me to choose at all, he took the draught
Of bitterness himself, and lightly quaffed
It off, and said the other one was mine.
And when I asked him what the deuce he meant
By doing that, he only looked at me   10
And smiled, and said it was a way of his.
And though I know the fellow, I have spent
Long time a-wondering when I shall be
As happy as Cliff Klingenhagen is.

5. *wormwood:* a bitter oil obtained from an herb.

Questions and Exercises

The first of these poems consists of a dialogue between two friends, one of whom is a poet (Terence was Housman's name for himself) and the other a person who objects to the kind of poetry his friend writes — "It gives a chap the belly-ache."

1. Who is speaking in the first fourteen lines? The remainder of the poem?

2. Why does the first speaker object to Terence's poetry? What kind of poetry does Terence write? What does line 13 tell us about this poetry?

3. What is meant by the lines "Malt does more than Milton can/To justify God's ways to man"? What does "malt" enable a person to do? Does the speaker of these lines really favor the "malt" way of dealing with life's problems? What are its disadvantages? What is meant by "Look into the pewter pot/To see the world as the world's not"?

4. What, according to the speaker in the third stanza, is life really like? Would you call this view pessimistic or realistic? Why should one "train for ill and not for good"? How does "the stuff I bring for sale" help one to "train for ill"? How can this "stuff" "friend you — In the dark and cloudy day"?

5. How did Mithridates "train for ill"? What is the connection between the story of Mithridates and the rest of the poem?

6. State the theme of this poem.

7. Why did Cliff Klingenhagen drink the glass of wormwood and leave the glass of wine for his friend? Why is Cliff happier than the speaker of the poem?

8. In what sense was Cliff "training for ill" in the same way Mithridates had? Compare the themes of these two poems.

THE LIFEGUARD

James Dickey

(1923–   )

In a stable of boats I lie still,
From all sleeping children hidden.
The leap of a fish from its shadow
Makes the whole lake instantly tremble.
With my foot on the water, I feel   5
The moon outside

Take on the utmost of its power.
I rise and go out through the boats.
I set my broad sole upon silver,
On the skin of the sky, on the moonlight,   10
Stepping outward from earth onto water
In quest of the miracle

This village of children believed
That I could perform as I dived
For one who had sunk from my sight.   15
I saw his cropped haircut go under.

I leapt, and my steep body flashed
Once, in the sun.

Dark drew all the light from my eyes.
Like a man who explores his death   20
By the pull of his slow-moving shoulders,
I hung head down in the cold,
Wide-eyed, contained, and alone
Among the weeds,

And my fingertips turned into stone   25
From clutching immovable blackness.
Time after time I leapt upward
Exploding in breath, and fell back
From the change in the children's faces
At my defeat.   30

Beneath them, I swam to the boathouse
With only my life in my arms
To wait for the lake to shine back
At the risen moon with such power
That my steps on the light of the ripples   35
Might be sustained.

Beneath me is nothing but brightness
Like the ghost of a snow field in summer.
As I move toward the center of the lake,
Which is also the center of the moon,   40
I am thinking of how I may be
The savior of one

Who has already died in my care.
The dark trees fade from around me.
The moon's dust hovers together.   45
I call softly out, and the child's
Voice answers through blinding water.
Patiently, slowly,

He rises, dilating to break
The surface of stone with his forehead.   50
He is one I do not remember
Having ever seen in his life.
The ground that I stand on is trembling
Upon his smile.

I wash the black mud from my hands.   55
On a light given off by the grave,
I kneel in the quick of the moon
At the heart of a distant forest
And hold in my arms a child
Of water, water, water.   60

Questions

Before exploring the theme of this poem, it is well to recognize its structure. Lines 1–15 describe the lifeguard's actions in the dramatic present; lines 16–36 are a flashback; lines 37 to the end resume the action with which the poem begins and launch into a kind of vision in which the lifeguard's actual experience is compared with, and fused with, his recognition of a spiritual reality.

1. What has already happened when the poem begins? How does the language of lines 19–26 suggest the lifeguard's experience in trying to rescue the drowning boy?

2. How does the lifeguard *feel* about what has happened? How do his actions reveal his feeling? What is the meaning of the "change in the children's faces"?

3. As the lifeguard wades toward the center of the lake (lines 37 and *ff.*), he is "thinking of how I may be/ The savior of one /Who has already died in my care." What child, in addition to the drowned one, is meant? How has he *died in my care*? Why does the lifeguard not remember ever having seen him alive? Why does the child "break the surface of *stone* with his forehead"? Why is he a child of *water*?

4. What event is suggested by the lifeguard's fantasy of walking on the water (lines 35–36)? by his conception of himself as a savior? What must the lifeguard do to "save" the (symbolic) child? What is the symbolic meaning of the mud on the lifeguard's hands?

5. How is the theme of the poem underscored by the contrast of moonlight with darkness?

STOPPING BY WOODS ON A SNOWY EVENING

Robert Frost

(1874–1963)

Whose woods these are I think I know.
His house is in the village though;
He will not see me stopping here
To watch his woods fill up with snow.

My little horse must think it queer   5
To stop without a farmhouse near
Between the woods and frozen lake
The darkest evening of the year.

He gives his harness bells a shake
To ask if there is some mistake.   10
The only other sound's the sweep
Of easy wind and downy flake.

The woods are lovely, dark and deep,
But I have promises to keep,
And miles to go before I sleep,   15
And miles to go before I sleep.

Questions and Exercises

1. There are three "characters" in this poem, the speaker, the horse, and the man who owns the woods. How do they differ in their attitude toward the woods? What three different ways of responding to a scene of natural beauty do the three characters represent?

2. Does the horse really "think it queer," or is this another way of bringing out the difference between man and animal? What is the horse "interested" in?

3. What attracts the man to the woods? How does this make him different from the horse and from the owner?

4. Why does the speaker say "But I have promises to keep"? What are these "promises"? What might he prefer to do?

5. Is "miles to go before I sleep" to be taken only literally, or does it suggest other meanings? What is gained by repeating this line? Does it take on larger implications the second time? Is there a connection between "sleeping" and the dark and deep woods?

DUST OF SNOW
Robert Frost

(1874–1963)

The way a crow
Shook down on me
The dust of snow
From a hemlock tree

Has given my heart   5
A change of mood
And saved some part
Of a day I had rued.*

8. *rued:* regretted.

BOY AT THE WINDOW
Richard Wilbur

(1921–   )

Seeing the snowman standing all alone
In dusk and cold is more than he can bear.
The small boy weeps to hear the wind prepare
A night of gnashings and enormous moan.
His tearful sight can hardly reach to where   5
The pale-faced figure with bitumen eyes
Returns him such a god-forsaken stare
As outcast Adam gave to Paradise.

The man of snow is, nonetheless, content,
Having no wish to go inside and die.   10
Still, he is moved to see the youngster cry.
Though frozen water is his element,
He melts enough to drop from one soft eye
A trickle of the purest rain, a tear
For the child at the bright pane surrounded by   15
Such warmth, such light, such love, and so
    much fear.

Questions and Exercises

Sometimes a poem's theme cannot be restated in general terms. The poem's "meaning" may be only a perception or an emotion which cannot be separated from the concrete terms in which it is stated in the poem. The poet tries to capture this perception or emotion in words and share it with us. The perception *is* the poem, the poem the perception.

In "Boy at the Window" Wilbur seems mainly interested in the *irony* of a small boy's tears over what he takes to be the sad plight of a snowman.

1. How does the poet reveal that the boy has humanized the snowman? Why does the boy feel sorry for the snowman?

2. Considering the snowman's "view" of the boy, what is the basic irony of the poem?
   a. Why is the snowman "content"? What different meanings can you find in "frozen water is his element"? in "melts"?
   b. Why does the snowman cry? What perception does he have of the boy's ironic plight?
   c. Is it really the snowman who has this perception? Who does? Does the speaker's attitude toward the little boy contain more than irony?

3. Why did Frost write the poem about a crow shaking snow out of a tree?

3

The Language of a Poem

In the last chapter we saw that a poem's theme is not the same as its subject, although the two are closely related, the theme growing out of the subject matter. It should also be clear by now that a poem's theme is by no means its total meaning but, like the subject matter, only one of the elements that make up the whole poem and that determine how we will receive it — that is, what the poem's overall effect on us will be. The theme, that is, cannot be isolated or extracted from the tissue of language that makes up the poem and gives it its special texture.

Actually, a poem's theme is affected by a number of other elements that will be discussed in this and later chapters: imagery, rhythm and meter, sound effects, the tone of voice of the poem's speaker, and the many devices of figurative language the poet uses to achieve concreteness and to convey meanings and associations that go beyond the literal. From this, it is clear that the theme does not give the poem its power; rather the poem gives power to the theme, makes us *feel* the theme on our pulse, so to speak.

Whatever a poem "means," then, it is first of all itself. Its *total meaning* comes about in large part from its *special uses of language*: its peculiar diction or choice of words, the evocative power of its images, the expressiveness of its figurative language. In this chapter we will deal with these things in order, calling in some new terms that will enable you to describe the workings of a poem with more accuracy and precision.

1. Diction

The diction of a poem is its distinctive vocabulary and the way its words are used to give the poem its special "flavor." Often this vocabulary helps us to define the speaker of the poem and his attitude toward the subject he is speaking about. If we go back to Hardy's "The Man He Killed" (page 32), we will see that the speaker of the poem defines himself as a member of the working class, a man without much formal education and not very much given to philosophical or political speculation. He does this not only by mentioning that he, like his foe in battle, had sold the tools of his trade (his "traps"), but through his diction. His use of such words and phrases as "old ancient inn," "wet right many a nipperkin," "shot him *dead*," "'list" (rather than enlist), "shoot a fellow down," and "help to half-a-crown" gives us a concrete sense of the man, his mind and his background, that somehow adds to our sympathy for his groping attempts to find an explanation for what he has done. This question might not baffle a more sophisticated man, yet the questions this simple man raises are fundamental; and his way of raising these questions is very much a part of the poem's "meaning."

If you go back and look at Frost's "Departmental" now, you will see how the gentle irony of the poem arises from its diction. What is the effect of such phrases as the following: "His business wasn't with such" (line 5), "put him onto the case" (line 12), the rhyming of *any* with *antennae, Formic* with *McCormic*, (lines 18 and 19, 22 and 23), *Janizary* (line 25), *atwiddle* (line 36), the use of *ungentle* and *departmental* in the last two lines?

No poem is unaffected by its diction, but let us turn now to some poems in which the diction plays a special, or controlling, role.

WE REAL COOL

Gwendolyn Brooks

(1917–   )

The Pool Players.
Seven at the Golden Shovel.

We real cool. We
Left school. We

Lurk late. We
Strike straight. We

Sing sin. We   5
Thin gin. We

Jazz June. We
Die soon.

Questions and Exercises

The diction of this poem cannot be entirely separated from its grammar, a further ingredient of meaning to be discussed in a later chapter. In the first line of the poem, for example, the slangy expression "real cool" is made still more slangy by the omission of the verb in the sentence.

1. Identify the words and expressions which give this poem a jazzy ring. Whom do you imagine to be the speaker of this poem?

2. Does the jazziness created by the poem's diction contribute to the irony of the last line? Explain.

3. How would you describe the overall tone of this poem, considering the degree of self-awareness indicated by the last line?

JANET WAKING

John Crowe Ransom

(1888–   )

Beautifully Janet slept
Till it was deeply morning. She woke then
And thought about her dainty-feathered hen,
To see how it had kept.

One kiss she gave her mother,   5
Only a small one gave she to her daddy
Who would have kissed each curl of his shining
  baby;
No kiss at all for her brother.

"Old Chucky, Old Chucky!" she cried,
Running on little pink feet upon the grass   10
To Chucky's house, and listening. But alas,
Her Chucky had died.

It was a transmogrifying* bee
Came droning down on Chucky's old bald head
And sat and put the poison. It scarcely bled,   15
But how exceedingly

And purply did the knot
Swell with the venom and communicate
Its rigor! Now the poor comb stood up straight
But Chucky did not.   20

So there was Janet
Kneeling on the wet grass, crying her brown hen
(Translated far beyond the daughters of men)
To rise and walk upon it.

And weeping fast as she had breath   25
Janet implored us, "Wake her from her sleep!"
And would not be instructed in how deep
Was the forgetful kingdom of death.

13. *transmogrifying:* grotesquely transforming.

Questions and Exercises

 This poem's lightness of tone is deceptive. Its skillful use of diction creates variations in moods that make us aware of how tragic the incident is for the little girl but enables us to see the tragedy from the point of view of the girl's father, who is the speaker of the poem (line 7 gives us information that only he could possess). The father's attitude toward his child and toward the event is humorously tender, since he is aware that this is the child's first encounter with the mystery of death. Thus the poem is a mixture of the grave and the gay.

1. What do the words *beautifully* (line 1) and *kept* (line 4) convey about Janet's naïveté and innocence? Keep in mind this idea, expressed also in the title, of Janet's *waking*.

2. What is the effect of the word *transmogrifying* in line 13?

3. Notice the contrast between "sat and put" and "But how exceedingly" in the same stanza. What is the purpose of this shift in diction? Why does the speaker use the scientific phrase "communicate its rigor" in line 18 and 19?

4. What is the tone of "Now the poor comb stood up straight/But Chucky did not"? Is it important to the effect that this line follow immediately after the scientific terminology of stanzas 4 and 5?

5. There are biblical echoes in the phrases "The daughters of men" and "To rise and walk upon it" in the next to last stanza. What effect does this growing dignity and solemnity of language have on our feelings (perhaps our fears) about Janet?

6. How is this almost comic event further dignified by the language of the last two lines? Is there irony in these lines, too? (For whom would death cause forgetfulness, in the adults' view? Why couldn't Janet be "instructed"?)

2. Imagery

Perhaps the thing most characteristic of poetry is that it *involves* us *in* an experience, an emotion, an attitude, an idea rather than merely telling us *about* these things. To do this it makes a direct appeal to our senses so that we can enter into, feel, and share with the poet whatever it is he wants to communicate. To do this, poetry relies heavily on *imagery*.

Basically an *image* is a word picture, the verbal equivalent of something we can actually see as if it were before our eyes in reality. Poetic imagery, however, often appeals to the other senses as well: sound, smell, taste, and touch — or the sense of hot and cold or the sense of hunger or fatigue or drowsiness, anything that has a *physical* origin.

It is important in reading poetry to allow your senses to engage fully in apprehending the images of the poem and to specify to yourself the sensations aroused by these images. Only then will you be able to grasp the relationship that joins the images of a poem together, the principle of order which underlies the images of the poem.

The following seven poems are of a special kind called *haiku,* a Japanese form of poetry which states a clear picture designed to convey a distinct emotion and arrive at a moment of intense insight. Every *haiku* has the same form: seventeen syllables in three lines of five, seven, and five syllables. Because they are simple and depend so largely for their effect on the precise choice of image, *haiku* make a good starting point for the understanding of imagery.

i

Clouds come from time to time —
and bring to men a chance to rest
from looking at the moon.

Matsuo Basho

(1644–1694)

ii

Grave mound, shake too!
My wailing voice —
the autumn wind.

Matsuo Basho

iii

The usually hateful crow:
he, too — this morning,
on the snow!

Matsuo Basho

iv

To cherry blooms I come,
   and under the blossoms go to sleep —
   no duties to be done!

                 Yosa Buson

                 (1716–1783)

v

As the spring rains fall,
   soaking in them, on the roof,
   is a child's rag ball.

                 Yosa Buson

vi

Blooms on the plum —
   and repentance for anger at people
   also has come.

                 Rosen

                 (1654–1733)

Questions

1. In *haiku* vi how do the associations of fresh plum blossoms, coming at the end of a long winter, relate to the idea of repentance? Is there an analogy between nature's repentance and man's?

2. See what associations and relationships you can discover in the other *haiku*. Can you express in your own words the nature of the "moment of truth" that the poet wished to capture? Is the "truth" separable from the mood? the mood from the image?

MEETING AT NIGHT

Robert Browning

(1812–1889)

The gray sea and the long black land;
And the yellow half-moon large and low;
And the startled little waves that leap
In fiery ringlets from their sleep,
As I gain the cove with pushing prow,   5
And quench its speed i' the slushy sand.

Then a mile of warm sea-scented beach;
Three fields to cross till a farm appears;
A tap at the pane, the quick sharp scratch
And blue spurt of a lighted match,   10
And a voice less loud, through its joys and fears,
Than the two hearts beating each to each!

PARTING AT MORNING

Robert Browning

Round the cape of a sudden came the sea,
And the sun looked over the mountain's rim:
And straight was a path of gold for him,
And the need of a world of men for me.

Questions and Exercises

"Meeting at Night" is a poem about the reunion of two lovers. In describing the last stretch of the journey of the lover as he goes to rejoin his sweetheart, the poet conveys his sense of urgency and anticipation entirely in terms of sense impressions — or images.

1. To what different senses do the images in this poem appeal?

2. In what way do lines 3 and 4 anticipate the picture painted in line 10? Do these images in some sense express the excitement and passion of the two lovers? Explain.

3. What does the poet gain by taking us with the lover as he travels "a mile of *warm sea-scented* beach" and crosses three fields? How do the "tap at the pane" and the "quick sharp scratch" convey the sense of *climax* to the journey?

4. Consider "Parting at Morning" as a sequel to "Meeting at Night." In what sense did the sea come "Round the cape of a sudden"? "Him" in line 3 refers to the sun. How does the picture of the sun's "path of gold" reinforce the emotion expressed in the last line?

5. In the light of the quality of the lover's experience described in "Meeting at Night," can you understand why he now feels "the need of a world of men"? Taken together, what do the two poems suggest about the experience of love?

WESTERN WIND

Anonymous

(16th century)

O western wind, when wilt thou blow
That the small rain down can rain?
Christ, that my love were in my arms,
And I in my bed again!

PIED BEAUTY

Gerard Manley Hopkins

(1844–1889)

Glory be to God for dappled things —
For skies of couple-color as a brinded cow;
For rose-moles all in stipple upon trout that
swim;
Fresh-firecoal chestnut-falls; finches' wings;

Landscape plotted and pieced — fold, fallow and
plow;   5
And all trades, their gear and tackle and trim.

All things counter, original, spare, strange;
Whatever is fickle, freckled (who knows how?)
With swift, slow; sweet, sour; adazzle, dim;
He fathers-forth whose beauty is past change: 10
Praise him.

Questions and Exercises

1. In "Western Wind" what connection is there between the speaker's
   desire for the western wind to bring the "small rain" and his desire
   to be passionately reunited with his sweetheart? What associations
   does rain have? Why "small rain"? Explain why you think the last
   two lines are, or are not, effective.

2. In "Pied Beauty" what do the images of the first stanza have in
   common?

3. How are these images related to the statement "With swift, slow;
   sweet, sour; adazzle, dim" in line 9? To the word *fickle* in line 8?
   Do all the images together generate enough feeling for the last line?
   Should the poem have ended with an exclamation mark? Why or
   why not?

3. Metaphor

With imagery, we are only a step away from the most funda-
mental principle of the language of poetry — the principle of
metaphor. *Metaphor* is the general term for figures of speech in
which one thing is compared to or identified with another thing
so that the emotional or imaginative qualities of the second "rub
off" on the first and invest it with those qualities. If the compari-
son is stated with a *like* or an *as*, it is called a *simile*; if the
comparison is only implied, it is called a metaphor. There are
several other kinds of metaphor (personification, synecdoche,
metonymy), but it is not as important to remember the names as
it is to understand how the principle of comparison works and
to see how these figures of speech help to express the full mean-
ing of the poem.

In approaching metaphors, don't be surprised to find that the two things being compared are seemingly widely dissimilar. Poets find unsuspected similarities in objects, and by thrusting the two objects together in comparison, they create a fresh image which shocks us into a new awareness of the original object. Actually, we are all poets at times: our daily speech is filled with metaphors, often unconscious. When we say about a girl "She's a *doll*," we are making an implied comparison and attributing certain qualities of prettiness and petiteness to the girl. Sometimes people invent new metaphors to convey an idea or an impression more vividly, but most of the metaphors we use in daily speech have been invented by someone else and have seen hard wear. If they have been used too much, they become clichés.

The poet, however, creates new metaphors out of his need to express a particular shade of meaning that will serve his overall purpose in the poem. His is a controlled use of metaphor. In "Dulce Et Decorum Est," (page 33) for instance, Owen describes the weary, pack-laden soldiers as "Bent double, *like* old beggars under sacks" not only because old beggars under sacks are more familiar to most people than weary soldiers struggling through sludge, but because the comparison is apt: both beggars and soldiers are dispossessed of their rights. More important, this comparison gives the plight of the soldiers precisely the emotional quality the poet wanted it to have: when he says that the soldiers limped on "bloodshod," he is implying a comparison between blood and shoes. Why is this metaphor more effective than the *literal* statement "They had bloody feet"?

In "Auto Wreck" (page 35) Shapiro devotes the first six lines of the poem to describing the arrival of the ambulance in terms that suggest a bird swooping down on its prey ("Wings in a heavy curve, dips down"), perhaps a vulture. He does this not simply for decoration or to make the ambulance's arrival more vivid but because such a comparison somehow contributes to the sense of the impersonality and unpredictability of human destruction which is an important part of the poem's meaning. Study the metaphors and similes in the last stanza of this poem and see if you can tell how they "work" and what they contribute to the poem's overall meaning.

The following poems demonstrate some interesting uses of metaphor.

To Lucasta, on Going to the Wars
Richard Lovelace

(1618–1658)

Tell me not, Sweet, I am unkind,
   That from the nunnery
Of thy chaste breast and quiet mind
   To war and arms I fly.

True, a new mistress now I chase,   5
   The first foe in the field;
And with a stronger faith embrace
   A sword, a horse, a shield.

Yet this inconstancy is such
   As you too shall adore;   10
I could not love thee, dear, so much,
   Loved I not honor more.

Arms and the Boy
Wilfred Owen

(1893–1918)

Let the boy try along this bayonet blade
How cold steel is, and keen with hunger of blood;
Blue with all malice, like a madman's flash;
And thinly drawn with famishing for flesh.

Lend him to stroke these blind, blunt bullet heads   5
Which long to nuzzle in the hearts of lads,
Or give him cartridges of fine zinc teeth,
Sharp with the sharpness of grief and death.

For his teeth seem for laughing round an apple.
There lurk no claws behind his fingers supple;   10
And God will grow no talons at his heels,
Nor antlers through the thickness of his curls.

THE GRAY SQUIRREL
Humbert Wolfe
(1885–1940)

Like a small gray
coffeepot
sits the squirrel.
He is not

all he should be,   5
kills by dozens
trees, and eats
his red-brown cousins.

The keeper, on the
other hand   10
, who shot him, is
a Christian, and

loves his enemies,
which shows
the squirrel was not   15
one of those.

THE BLOODY SIRE
Robinson Jeffers
(1887–1962)

It is not bad. Let them play.
Let the guns bark and the bombing-plane
Speak his prodigious blasphemies.

It is not bad, it is high time,
Stark violence is still the sire of all the world's values.   5

What but the wolf's tooth whittled so fine
The fleet limbs of the antelope?
What but fear winged the birds and hunger
Gemmed with such eyes the great goshawk's head?
Violence has been the sire of all the world's values.   10

Who would remember Helen's face
Lacking the terrible halo of spears?
Who formed Christ but Herod and Caesar,
The cruel and bloody victories of Caesar?
Violence has been the sire of all the world's values.   15

Never weep, let them play,
Old violence is not too old to beget new values.

Questions and Exercises

1. In "To Lucasta, on Going to the Wars" why does the poet refer to Lucasta's "chaste breast and quiet mind" as a "nunnery"? ("Chaste breast and quiet mind," by the way is itself an example of a kind of metaphor called a *synecdoche,* in which the part stands for the whole. Why does he single out these particular parts of his sweetheart to say good-bye to?)

2. Who is the soldier's "new mistress"? This comparison now shapes the language and meaning of the balance of the poem. How does it explain the use of *embrace* in line 7? of *inconstancy* in line 9?

3. In "Arms and the Boy" to what are the bullets being compared in lines 5 and 6? Why is the comparison *ironic*? In what sense are grief and death like cartridges?

4. To what is the boy contrasted in lines 10 and 11?

5. Is the comparison of the squirrel to a coffeepot apt? How does this comparison influence our view of the squirrel? of the keeper?

6. The key to understanding "The Bloody Sire" is to understand how violence can be "the sire of all the world's values" (a statement that seems contradictory but which is a *paradox*) and to relate the individual details in the poem to this general statement. The details are all expressed as metaphors.

Except for the first stanza, whose concluding statement depends on the "proof" provided in the other stanzas, the details are all examples of values that have been "sired" by violence.

In what sense did the wolf "whittle" the limbs of the antelope, and how did fear "wing" the birds and hunger "gem" the head of the goshawk?

7. Stanza three makes use of four *allusions*. An allusion is a reference to some historical or biblical or mythological person or thing or to anything that is part of the public knowledge or heritage. It is a kind of metaphor and is used by a poet to bring into his poem, with one quick stroke, a body of information with rich associations for anyone who is familiar with his cultural heritage.

   a. Who was Helen? In what sense did she have a "halo of spears"? Why a "halo"?

   b. How did Herod and Caesar help to "form" Christ? How is this an example of violence "siring" the world's values?

Full Many a Glorious Morning

William Shakespeare

(1564–1616)

Full many a glorious morning have I seen
Flatter the mountain tops with sovereign eye,
Kissing with golden face the meadows green,
Gilding pale streams with heavenly alchemy;
Anon permit the basest clouds to ride   5
With ugly rack on his celestial face,
And from the forlorn world his visage hide,
Stealing unseen to west with this disgrace:

Even so my sun one early morn did shine
With all-triumphant splendor on my brow;   10
But out, alack! he was but one hour mine;
The region cloud hath masked him from me now.
Yet him for this my love no whit disdaineth;
Suns of the world may stain when heaven's sun
        staineth.

4. *alchemy:* the turning of base metals into gold.

On His Blindness

John Milton

(1608–1674)

When I consider how my light is spent,
  Ere half my days in this dark world and wide,
  And that one talent which is death to hide*
  Lodged with me useless, though my soul more bent
To serve therewith my Maker, and present   5
  My true account, lest he returning chide;
  "Doth God exact day-labor, light denied?"
  I fondly* ask. But Patience, to prevent
That murmur, soon replies, "God doth not need
  Either man's work or his own gifts; who best   10
  Bear his mild yoke, they serve him best. His state
Is kingly: thousands* at his bidding speed
  And post o'er land and ocean without rest;
  They also serve who only stand and wait."

3. *talent . . . hide:* See Matt. 25:14–30. 8. *fondly:* foolishly. 12. *thousands:* thousands of angels.

On First Looking into Chapman's Homer*

John Keats

(1795–1821)

Much have I traveled in the realms of gold,
  And many goodly states and kingdoms seen;
  Round many western islands have I been

* George Chapman was a sixteenth-century playwright and poet who made a famous translation of Homer's *Iliad* and *Odyssey*. When Keats read Chapman's translation, it was as if Homer's literary works were being opened up to him for the first time. It was like making a new discovery.

Which bards in fealty to Apollo hold.*
Oft of one wide expanse had I been told   5
That deep-browed Homer ruled as his demesne;*
Yet did I never breathe its pure serene
Till I heard Chapman speak out loud and bold.
Then felt I like some watcher of the skies
When a new planet swims into his ken;*   10
Or like stout Cortez* when with eagle eyes
He stared at the Pacific — and all his men
Looked at each other with a wild surmise —
Silent, upon a peak in Darien.*

4. *in fealty . . . hold:* hold in faithfulness to Apollo.   6. *demesne:* domain.
10. *ken:* range of vision.   11. *Cortez:* conqueror of Mexico. Actually,
Balboa was the first European to see the Pacific Ocean.   14. *Darien:* the
isthmus of Panama.

The three preceding poems illustrate a form called the *sonnet.*
There are two kinds of sonnets, the Shakespearean and the Italian
or Petrarchan. Both kinds have fourteen lines, but the lines are
grouped in slightly different ways, and the pattern of rhyming is
different.

The Shakespearean sonnet consists of three groups of four
lines (each of these groups called a *quatrain*) and a pair of rhym-
ing lines (called a *couplet*) at the end. If you put a letter of the
alphabet after each new rhyme or sound, the *rhyme scheme* can
be described as follows: *a b a b, c d c d, e f e f, g g.* All of the lines
have the same number of heavily stressed syllables (five) and
essentially the same beat (one unstressed syllable followed by a
stressed syllable).

The Italian sonnet consists of two quatrains (together called
the *octave*) and a six line "conclusion" (called a *sestet*). The
lines of the two quatrains (the octave) rhyme as follows: *a b b a,
a b b a.* The lines of the sestet can rhyme in a number of different
ways. The lines have the same number of stressed and unstressed
syllables and the same "beat" as the Shakespearean sonnet.

A knowledge of the sonnet's *structure* is useful for breaking
the poem into its component parts and seeing how they work
together.

Questions and Exercises

1. In the first quatrain of "Full Many a Glorious Morning," to what is the sun being compared? How do you know?

2. In what sense are the streams gilded with "alchemy"?

3. How is the sun "disgraced" in the second quatrain? What is an "ugly rack"? How does the idea of the sun's "disgrace" follow from the way the sun is characterized in the first quatrain?

4. In the third quatrain the poet begins to compare the scene described in the first two quatrains to something that has happened between himself and a friend. In other words the first two quatrains become a *metaphor* for what he wants to say in the last six lines.
   a. Who is "my sun" in line 9? In what sense did he "shine with all-triumphant splendor on my brow"?
   b. What happened to "my sun"? To what (or whom) does "the region cloud" refer?
   c. Why does the speaker say that in spite of what has happened he still loves his friend? How does the last line link the last six lines to the first eight lines?

5. What kind of sonnet is "On His Blindness"?
   The word *talent* in line 3 is an allusion, a pun, and a metaphor. It alludes, first, to the New Testament story of the servant who failed to use the talent (money) entrusted to him by his master and thereby lost all that he had been given. How does it relate to the word *spent* in line 1? How does this allusion enrich the meaning of the quatrain?

6. The word *Patience* (notice the capital) is a kind of metaphor called a *personification*, a poetic device in which an abstract concept is given human characteristics, such as the ability to speak. State in your own words the reply given by Patience to the speaker's question. Relate this reply to the first eight lines of the poem. Are there really two characters here, or does this dialogue represent an inner conflict in the speaker?

7. What is the connection between the parable alluded to in line 3 and the "meaning" of the whole poem?

8. The phrase "traveled in the realms of gold" in line 1 is a metaphor. To what physical activity does it refer? What are the "goodly states," the "kingdoms," the "western islands"? Why does Keats use this particular metaphor? Why do bards "hold fealty" to Apollo?

9. What was the "wide expanse" ruled over by Homer? How might

a "watcher of the skies" feel "when a new planet swims into his ken"?

10. Historically, Balboa, not Cortez, discovered the Pacific. Does this historical inaccuracy matter in this poem? Explain in your own words the emotion Keats is trying to express in the last four lines about his reading of Chapman's Homer.

The following three poems rely heavily on metaphor for feeling and for richness of suggestion. In reading them, be aware of the larger metaphor underlying each as well as the individual metaphors within the lines.

THE NET
Sara Teasdale
(1884–1933)

I made you many and many a song,
   Yet never one told all you are —
It was as though a net of words
   Were flung to catch a star;

It was as though I curved my hand   5
   And dipped sea-water eagerly,
Only to find it lost the blue
   Dark splendor of the sea.

ON MY FIRST SON
Ben Jonson
(1573?–1637)

Farewell, thou child of my right hand, and joy;
My sin was too much hope of thee, loved boy.
Seven years thou wast lent to me, and I thee pay,
Exacted by thy fate, on the just day.
O, I could lose all father now. For why   5
Will man lament the state he should envy?

To have so soon 'scaped the world's, and flesh's, rage.
And if no other misery, yet age?
Rest in soft peace, and, asked, say here doth lie
Ben Jonson, his best piece of poetry.   10
For whose sake, henceforth, all his vows be such,
As what he loves may never like too much.

Nothing Gold Can Stay

Robert Frost

(1874–1963)

Nature's first green is gold,
Her hardest hue to hold.
Her early leaf's a flower;
But only so an hour.
Then leaf subsides to leaf.   5
So Eden sank to grief,
So dawn goes down to day.
Nothing gold can stay.

Exercise

Try writing a paraphrase of one of the preceding poems. Compare
the paraphrase with the original. What is lost?

4

The Poem and Its Speaker

In the discussion so far, we have often referred to the "speaker" of a poem, rather than to the poet himself. That is because in almost every poem the poet creates a special "character" (sometimes called the *persona*) who can be imagined saying the words which the poet sets down. This "speaker" speaks with his own unique "voice," depending upon his personality, his background, and his attitude toward the thing he is speaking about. This "voice" then becomes an integral part of the poem's meaning, signaling to the reader how he is to "take" the words of the poem.

Sometimes the speaker is evidently the poet himself, as is the case with Ben Jonson's "On My First Son" (page 64) and with John Milton's "On His Blindness" (page 61): we know that Milton did go blind at a certain point in his career. We also know that John Keats composed "On First Looking into Chapman's Homer" the same night on which a friend had read the Chapman translation aloud to him. Nevertheless, even when the poet himself is clearly the speaker, he can speak with many "voices," just as we all speak with several different voices in the course of a day, depending on our mood, the subject we are speaking about and the person to whom we are speaking: the milkman, the boss, our wife, a child, the umpire, the teacher. None of us is only one person. So with the poet; he can adopt a different role, or *persona*, for each of the many different occasions on which he "speaks" to us through his poems.

Many poems, of course, have speakers who are clearly *not* the poet himself. In the anonymous ballad "The Twa Corbies" (page 4) all but the first three lines are spoken by one of the crows. Our knowledge of who the speaker is, what his attitude is toward the slain knight (so much meat!), and what he intends to do invests his words with a peculiar horror and affects the tone and meaning of the whole poem. Clearly, too, the speaker in Thomas Hardy's "The Man He Killed" (page 32), with his ungrammatical expressions, is not the same as the learned and highly literate poet and novelist who created him. Neither, of course, can Amy Lowell be confused with the speaker, the "I," of "Patterns" (page 11), an eighteenth-century woman whose grief and disappointment cause her to burst out at the end with "Christ! What are patterns for?" Such poems, called monologues, can become highly dramatic when we realize that the speaker is speaking to a specific audience, as in Tennyson's "Ulysses" (page 112) and Browning's "My Last Duchess" (page 119).

In most poems, however, the speaker is neither the poet himself nor a clearly defined character in the drama which is the poem. He is defined by the diction of the poem, by the imagery, the rhythms, the sounds, and even the grammar — all the things that give the speaker his special tone of voice (angry, amused, sad, solemn, sarcastic, bitter, loving) — and it is only by attending closely to these things that you will discover "who" the speaker is. We saw that in John Crowe Ransom's "Janet Waking" (page 48), the speaker turned out to be Janet's father and that his special way of viewing and expressing Janet's tragedy was an important element in our experience of the poem.

Consider the role of the speaker in the following poems. Remember that the speaker and his voice cannot be considered apart from the other elements of poetry that you have already studied (diction, imagery, figurative language) and some that you will study later (rhythm, sound, grammar).

WITHOUT BENEFIT OF DECLARATION
Langston Hughes

(1902–1967)

Listen here, Joe,
Don't you know
That tomorrow
You got to go

Out yonder where   5
The steel winds blow?

Listen here, kid,
It's been said
Tomorrow you'll be dead
Out there where   10
The snow is lead.

Don't ask me why.
Just go ahead and die.
Hidden from the sky
Out yonder you'll lie: 15
A medal to your family —
In exchange for
A guy.

Mama, don't cry.

Questions and Exercises

1. Describe the speaker's tone of voice in this poem. What can you tell about the speaker?
2. What are the "steel winds" and how is it that "The snow is lead"?
3. Explain the relation between the title and the rest of the poem.

MY PAPA'S WALTZ

Theodore Roethke

(1908–1963)

The whiskey on your breath
Could make a small boy dizzy;
But I hung on like death:
Such waltzing was not easy.

We romped until the pans   5
Slid from the kitchen shelf;

My mother's countenance
Could not unfrown itself.

The hand that held my wrist
Was battered on one knuckle;   10
At every step you missed
My right ear scraped a buckle.

You beat time on my head
With a palm caked hard by dirt,
Then waltzed me off to bed   15
Still clinging to your shirt.

Questions and Exercises

1. Is the speaker of this poem a small boy or a grown man? How do you know?

2. What is the condition of the papa? Why is what he is doing called a waltz?

3. If the "mother's countenance / Could not unfrown itself" why did she not try to stop the proceedings?

4. If there is a "double vision" in this poem, that of the small boy and that of the grown man, what is the difference in the way they view the incident?

SONNET TO MY MOTHER

George Barker

(1913–   )

Most near, most dear, most loved and most far,
Under the window where I often found her
Sitting as huge as Asia, seismic* with laughter,
Gin and chicken helpless in her Irish hand,
Irresistible as Rabelais* but most tender for   5
The lame dogs and hurt birds that surround her —
She is a procession no one can follow after
But be like a little dog following a brass band.

3. *seismic:* earthshaking.   5. *Rabelais:* satirical French author
(1494?–1553).

She will not glance up at the bomber or condescend
To drop her gin and scuttle to a cellar,
But lean on the mahogany table like a mountain   10
Whom only faith can move, and so I send
O all my faith and all my love to tell her
That she will move from mourning into morning.

Questions and Exercises

1. For what specific qualities does the speaker love and respect his
   mother? How does she differ from the conventional mother that
   would be addressed on a Mother's Day card? How is she particu-
   larized?

2. What lines best describe her capacity for loving and being loved?

3. Describe the kind of love she inspires in her son. Is he at all ashamed
   of her? What is his tone of voice in the poem?

4. How does this poem differ from the traditional Italian sonnet?

BREDON HILL

A. E. Housman

(1859–1936)

In summertime on Bredon
   The bells they sound so clear;
Round both the shires they ring them
   In steeples far and near,
   A happy noise to hear.   5

Here of a Sunday morning
   My love and I would lie,
And see the colored counties,
   And hear the larks so high
   About us in the sky.   10

The bells would ring to call her
  In valleys miles away:
"Come all to church, good people;
  Good people, come and pray."
  But here my love would stay.   15

And I would turn and answer
  Among the springing thyme,
"Oh, peal upon our wedding,
  And we will hear the chime,
  And come to church in time."   20

But when the snows at Christmas
  On Bredon top were strown,
My love rose up so early
  And stole out unbeknown
  And went to church alone.   25

They tolled the one bell only,
  Groom there was none to see,
The mourners followed after,
  And so to church went she,
  And would not wait for me.   30

The bells they sound on Bredon,
  And still the steeples hum.
"Come all to church, good people, — "
  Oh, noisy bells, be dumb;
  I hear you, I will come.   35

Questions and Exercises

1. Who is the speaker of this poem? Where is he?
2. How does the tone of voice in lines 1–20 differ from that in the last two lines? Account for this change.

ANTHEM FOR DOOMED YOUTH

Wilfred Owen

(1893–1918)

What passing-bells for these who die as cattle?
Only the monstrous anger of the guns.
Only the stuttering rifles' rapid rattle
Can patter out their hasty orisons.*
No mockeries for them; no prayers nor bells,   5
Nor any voice of mourning save the choirs, —
The shrill, demented choirs of wailing shells;
And bugles calling for them from sad shires.

What candles may be held to speed them all?
Not in the hands of boys, but in their eyes   10
Shall shine the holy glimmers of good-byes.
The pallor of girls' brows shall be their pall;
Their flowers the tenderness of patient minds,
And each slow dusk a drawing-down of blinds.

4. *orisons:* prayers.

Questions and Exercises

1. How do the words *cattle, monstrous, hasty, mockeries, shrill,* and
   demented define the tone of the octave?

2. Do you notice a change of tone in the last line of the octave? Is this
   change of tone carried on in the sestet? Account for this change.

3. Explain the metaphor that underlies the entire octave. How does this
   metaphor contribute to the tone?

4. There are four metaphors in the sestet. Explain how "glimmers" in
   their eyes" and "pallor of girls' brows" are related to "candles" and
   "pall." What metaphors are used for "flowers?" Do all these meta-
   phors serve to reinforce a single tone?

IN WESTMINSTER ABBEY*

John Betjeman

(1906–   )

Let me take this other glove off
  As the *vox humana** swells,
And the beauteous Fields of Eden
  Bask beneath the Abbey bells.
Here, where England's statesmen lie,   5
Listen to a lady's* cry.

Gracious Lord, oh bomb the Germans.
  Spare their women for Thy Sake,
And if that is not too easy
  We will pardon Thy Mistake.   10
But, gracious Lord, whate'er shall be,
Don't let anyone bomb me.

Keep our Empire undismembered,
  Guide our Forces by Thy Hand,
Gallant blacks from far Jamaica,   15
  Honduras and Togoland;
Protect them Lord in all their fights,
And, even more, protect the whites.

Think of what our Nation stands for,
  Books from Boots'* and country lanes,   20
Free speech, free passes, class distinction,
  Democracy and proper drains.
Lord, put beneath Thy special care
One-eighty-nine Cadogan Square.*

* Westminster Abbey in London is the most famous of English cathe-
drals; it is also the burial place of royalty, statesmen, writers, and so on.
2. *vox humana:* literally, "human voice"; a setting of the reeds on a pipe
organ that imitates the human voice.   6. *a lady's:* the speaker's.
20. *Boots':* a London bookstore.   26. *One-eighty-nine Cadogan Square:* the
lady's fashionable address.

Although dear Lord I am a sinner,   25
   I have done no major crime;
Now I'll come to Evening Service
   Whensoever I have the time.
So, Lord, reserve for me a crown,
And do not let my shares go down.   30

I will labor for Thy Kingdom,
   Help our lads to win the war,
Send white feathers to the cowards,
   Join the Women's Army Corps,
Then wash the Steps around Thy Throne   35
In the Eternal Safety Zone.

Now I feel a little better,
   What a treat to hear Thy Word,
Where the bones of leading statesmen,
   Have so often been interred.   40
And now, dear Lord, I cannot wait
Because I have a luncheon date.

Questions and Exercises

1. The speaker of this poem is a hypocritical British lady of fashion. Describe her many hypocrisies.

2. By allowing the lady to speak for herself, the poet makes some sharp criticisms of the British upper class. But would a lady of her position really speak this way, or is there "conspiracy" between the poet himself and the lady he has created? Explain.

NEGRO HERO
For Dorie Miller
Gwendolyn Brooks

(1917–   )

I had to kick their law into their teeth in order to save
   them.
However I have heard that sometimes you have to deal

Devilishly with drowning men in order to swim them
    to shore.
Or they will haul themselves and you to the trash and
    the fish beneath.
(When I think of this, I do not worry about a few   5
Chipped teeth.)

It is good I gave glory, it is good I put gold on their
    name.
Or there would have been spikes in the afterward
    hands.
But let us speak only of my success and the pictures in
    the Caucasian dailies
As well as the Negro weeklies. For I am a gem.   10
(They are not concerned that it was hardly The Enemy
    my fight was against
But them.)

It was a tall time. And of course my blood was
Boiling about in my head and straining and howling
    and singing me on.
Of course I was rolled on wheels of my boy itch to get
    at the gun.   15
Of course all the delicate rehearsal shots of my child-
    hood massed in mirage before me.
Of course I was child
And my first swallow of the liquor of battle bleeding
    black air dying and demon noise
Made me wild.

It was kinder than that, though, and I showed like a
    banner my kindness.   20
I loved. And a man will guard when he loves.
Their white-gowned democracy was my fair lady.
With her knife lying cold, straight, in the softness
    of her sweet-flowing sleeve.
But for the sake of the dear smiling mouth and the stut-
    tered promise I toyed with my life.

I threw back! — I would not remember   25
Entirely the knife.

Still — am I good enough to die for them, is my blood
    bright enough to be spilled,
Was my constant back-question — are they clear
On this? Or do I intrude even now?
Am I clean enough to kill for them, do they wish me to   30
    kill
For them or is my place while death licks his lips and
    strides to them
In the galley still?

(In a southern city a white man said
Indeed, I'd rather be dead;
Indeed, I'd rather be shot in the head   35
Or ridden to waste on the back of a flood
Than saved by the drop of a black man's blood.)

Naturally, the important thing is, I helped to save
    them, them and a part of their democracy.
Even if I had to kick their law into their teeth in order to
    do that for them.
And I am feeling well and settled in myself because I
    believe it was a good job,   40
Despite this possible horror: that they might prefer the
Preservation of their law in all its sick dignity and
    their knives
To the continuation of their creed
And their lives.

    Dorie Miller was a Negro sailor serving as a cook on a battle-
ship at Pearl Harbor on December 7, 1941. When the Japanese
planes attacked, he manned one of the anti-aircraft guns (though
he hadn't been trained for this job) and shot down several planes.
He was awarded the Navy Cross for his heroism.

Questions and Exercises

1. Since the poet who wrote this poem is a woman, the voice we hear cannot be her own. The speaker is obviously Dorie Miller. Describe the tone of voice you hear in the first stanza. What words and phrases best define this tone of voice?

2. Explain the metaphor "you have to 'deal devilishly with drowning men . . ." (line 4).

3. What shift in the tone of voice do you hear in lines 9 and 10? Does the tone of voice shift again in the third stanza? Explain. Explain how line 18 achieves the effect of putting us in the midst of battle.

4. In what sense is democracy a white-gowned lady with a knife up her sleeve?

5. Explain how Miller had to "kick their law into their teeth" in order to save them. What fear is expressed in the last three lines?

6. Write a paragraph stating the theme of this poem.

BALLAD OF FINE DAYS

Phyllis McGinley

(1905–   )

"Temperatures have soared to almost summer levels . . . making conditions ideal for bombing offensives."
— *Excerpt from B.B.C. news broadcast.*

All in the summery weather,
  To east and south and north,
The bombers fly together
  And the fighters squire them forth.

While the lilac bursts in flower   5
  And buttercups brim with gold,
Hour by lethal hour,
  Now fiercer buds unfold.

For the storms of springtime lessen,
  The meadow lures the bee,   10

And there blooms tonight in Essen
    What bloomed in Coventry.

All in the summery weather,
    Fleeter than swallows fare,
The bombers fly together   15
    Through the innocent air.

THE CONQUERORS

Phyllis McGinley

It seems vainglorious and proud
Of Atom-man to boast aloud
    His prowess homicidal
When one remembers how for years,
With their rude stones and humble spears,   5
Our sires, at wiping out their peers,
    Were almost never idle.

Despite his under-fissioned art
The Hittite made a splendid start
    Toward smiting lesser nations;   10
While Tamerlane, it's widely known,
Without a bomb to call his own
    Destroyed whole populations.

Nor did the ancient Persian need
Uranium to kill his Mede,   15
    The Viking earl, his foeman.
The Greeks got excellent results
With swords and engined catapults.
    A chariot served the Roman.

Mere cannon garnered quite a yield   20
On Waterloo's tempestuous field.
    At Hastings and at Flodden

Stout countrymen, with just a bow
And arrow, laid their thousands low.
   And Gettysburg was sodden.   25

Though doubtless now our shrewd machines
Can blow the world to smithereens
   More tidily and so on,
Let's give our ancestors their due.
Their ways were coarse, their weapons few.   30
But ah! how wondrously they slew
   With what they had to go on.

Questions and Exercises

1. Explain how the tone as well as the theme of "Ballad of Fine Days" depends on the *ironic* contrast between the time of year and what is actually happening.

2. Explain the metaphor "Now fiercer buds unfold," line 8.

3. What "bloomed" in Coventry? Why "bloomed"? Where is Essen?

4. "The Conquerors" is another example of how a serious subject can be treated in a light or mocking voice. Describe the tonal effect of rhyming *homicidal* with *idle* in the first stanza. What is the effect of juxtaposing the word *sires* with the colloquial expression "*wiping out* their peers"?

5. Describe the effect of "splendid start" and "without a bomb to call their own" in the second stanza. Is the latter expression a cliché? How does "excellent results" affect the tone of stanza three? Is this an understatement?

6. Compare the tone of these two poems.

CHANNEL FIRING

Thomas Hardy

(1840–1928)

That night your great guns, unawares,
Shook all our coffins as we lay,

And broke the chancel window-squares,
We thought it was the Judgment-day

And sat upright. While drearisome   5
Arose the howl of wakened hounds:
The mouse let fall the altar-crumb,
The worms drew back into the mounds,

The glebe cow* drooled. Till God called, "No;
It's gunnery practice out at sea   10
Just as before you went below;
The world is as it used to be:

"All nations striving strong to make
Red war yet redder. Mad as hatters
They do no more for Christés* sake   15
Than you who are helpless in such matters.

"That this is not the judgment hour
For some of them's a blessed thing,
For if it were they'd have to scour
Hell's floor for so much threatening . . .   20

"Ha, ha. It will be warmer when
I blow the trumpet (if indeed
I ever do; for you are men,
And rest eternal sorely need)."

So down we lay again. "I wonder,   25
Will the world ever saner be,"
Said one, "than when He sent us under
In our indifferent century!"

---

9. *glebe cow:* glebe refers to land belonging to a parish church; the cow
also belongs to the church.   15. *Christés:* Middle English spelling.

And many a skeleton shook his head.
"Instead of preaching forty year," 30
My neighbor Parson Thirdly said,
"I wish I had stuck to pipes and beer."

Again the guns disturbed the hour,
Roaring their readiness to avenge,
As far inland as Stourton Tower,* 35
And Camelot* and starlit Stonehenge.*

35. **Stourton Tower:** a tower in Wiltshire, England, commemorating King Alfred's successes against Danish invaders in the ninth century.
36. **Camelot:** King Arthur's castle and court. **Stonehenge:** ancient ruins on Salisbury Plain in England.

Questions and Exercises

1. Who is the speaker in lines 1–9? Where is he? To whom is he speaking? What is his tone of voice? Point out the details that establish this tone.

2. In lines 9–24 the speaker is God. He has read the first speaker's thoughts. Compare the tone of God's reply to the first speaker's tone. Point out the words and phrases that establish God's tone of voice.

3. What other speakers appear in lines 25–29 and 30–32? Why do they speak as they do?

4. In the last stanza there is a fifth speaker, someone closely identifiable with the poet himself. Describe the complete change of tone that comes in this stanza.

5. What do Stourton Tower, Camelot, and Stonehenge all have in common? How does this relationship express the poem's theme? The name "Christ" is given its Middle English spelling, "Christés." How does this tie in with the theme of the poem?

6. Is the poem, finally, humorous or serious?

7. Compare the theme of this poem with that of "The Conquerors" and "Ballad of Fine Days." What differences in *tone* do you notice?

The Umpire

Walker Gibson

(1919–   )

Everyone knows he's blind as a bat.
Besides, it's tricky to decide,
As ball meets mitt with a loud splat,
Whether it curved an inch outside
Or just an inch the other way   5
For a called strike. But anyway,
Nobody thinks that just because
Instead he calls that close one Ball,
That that was what it really *was*.
(The pitcher doesn't agree at all.)   10
His eyes are weak, his vision's blurred,
He can't tell a strike from a barn door —
And yet we have to take his word:
The pitch that was something else before
(And that's the mystery no one knows)   15
Has gotten to be a ball by now,
Or got to be called ball, anyhow.
All this explains why, I suppose,
People like to watch baseball games,
Where Things are not confused with Names.   20

Questions and Exercises

1. At first this poem seems no more than a piece of light verse on the subject of "blind" umpires. But the last line introduces a serious philosophical and semantic problem. What *is* this problem? How is the statement in the last line prepared for in lines 7–10 and line 17?

2. Still, the poem is light in tone, though very skillfully controlled. There are two clichés in the poem. What are they? Whose "voice" is represented by the clichés? What effect did the poet want to achieve by using these clichés? What other "voice" dominates the poem? Is the real speaker a person who is likely to be given to using seriously such expressions as "He can't tell a strike from a barn door"?

Two Jazz Poems

Carl Wendell Hines, Jr.

(1940–   )

#1

yeah here am i
am standing
at the crest of a tallest
hill with a trumpet
in my hand & dark   5
glasses
on.
   bearded & bereted i proudly stand!
     but there are no eyes to see me.
   i send down cool sounds!   10
     but there are no ears to hear me.
   my lips they quiver in aether-emptiness!
     there are no hearts to love me.
surely though through night's gray fog mist
of delusion & dream   15
& the rivers of tears that flow
like gelatin soul-juice
some apathetic bearer of
paranoidic peyote visions (or some
other source of inspiration) shall   20
   hear the song i play. shall
   see the beard & beret. shall
   become inflamed beyond all hope
with emotion's everlasting fire
& join me   25
   in
     eternal
        Peace.
& but yet well
who knows?   30

#2

there he stands. see?
like a black Ancient Mariner his
wrinkled old face so
full of the wearies of living is
turned downward with   5
closed eyes. his frayed-collar
faded-blue old shirt turns
dark with sweat & the old
necktie undone drops
loosely about the worn   10
old jacket see? just
barely holding his
sagging stomach in. yeah.
his run-down shoes have
paper in them & his   15
rough unshaven face shows
pain
in each wrinkle.

but there he stands. in
self-brought solitude head   20
still down eyes
still closed ears
perked & trained upon
the bass line for
across his chest lies an old   25
alto saxophone —
supported from his neck by
a wire coat hanger.

gently he lifts it now
to parted lips. to   30
tell all the world that
he is a Black Man. that
he was sent here to preach
the Black Gospel of Jazz.

now preaching it with words of 35
screaming notes & chords he
is no longer a man. no not even
a Black Man. but (yeah!)
a Bird! —
one that gathers his wings & flies 40
  high
    high
      higher
until he flies away! or
comes back to find himself 45
a Black Man
again.

Questions and Exercises

1. In the first poem, account for the difference between the tone of the build-up and the tone of the last two lines. Why did the poet put the words "in eternal Peace" on separate lines?

2. In the second poem, who is the man being described? How does the speaker feel about him? Explain the simile and the allusion "like a black Ancient Mariner."

3. How does the old man "tell all the world that he is a Black Man"? Describe the speaker's feeling about this "telling." How does the old man become a bird?

4. Explain the sudden change of tone in the last three lines.

THE SAVAGE BEAST
William Carlos Williams
(1883–1963)

As I leaped to retrieve
my property
he leaped with all his weight
so that I felt

the wind of his jaws 5
as his teeth gnashed

before my mouth.
Isn't he awful! said

the woman, his collar
straining under her clutch.   10
Yes, I replied drily
wanting to eviscerate

the thing there, scoop
out his brains
and eat them — and hers   15
too! Until it flashed

on me, How many, like
this dog, could I not wish
had been here in my
place, only a little closer!   20

APPARENTLY WITH NO SURPRISE

Emily Dickinson

(1830–1886)

Apparently with no surprise
To any happy Flower
The Frost beheads it at its play —
In accidental power —
The blonde Assassin passes on —   5
The Sun proceeds unmoved
To measure off another Day
For an Approving God.

Questions and Exercises

1. Who is really the "savage beast" in Williams' poem?
2. Discuss the honesty of the speaker.

3. "Apparently with No Surprise" derives much of its power from its tone of horror. How is this tone established? What is the effect of "beheads" in line 3? of the fact that the assassin is "blonde"? What comment does this poem make on the kind of universe we live in?

To an American Poet Just Dead

Richard Wilbur

(1921–   )

In the *Boston Sunday Herald* just three lines
Of no-point type for you who used to sing
The praises of imaginary wines,
And died, or so I'm told, of the real thing.

Also gone, but a lot less forgotten,   5
Are an eminent cut-rate druggist, a lover of giving,
A lender, and various brokers; gone from this rotten
Taxable world to a higher standard of living.

It is out in the comfy suburbs I read you are dead,
And the soupy summer is settling, full of the yawns   10
Of Sunday fathers loitering late in bed,
And the ssshh of sprays on all the little lawns.

Will the sprays weep wide for you their chaplet* tears?
For you will deep-freeze units melt and mourn?
For you will Studebakers shred their gears   15
And sound from each garage a muted horn?

They won't. In summer sunk and stupefied
The suburbs deepen in their sleep of death.
And though they sleep the sounder since you died
It's just as well that now you save your breath.   20

---

13. *chaplet:* like a string of beads.

Questions and Exercises

1. Identify the speaker of this poem — the sort of man he is, where he
   lives. What is his attitude toward his neighbors? Toward poets?
   Toward cut-rate druggists, lovers of giving, lenders, brokers? How
   do you know? Consider the following:
   a. How does the pun on "no-point type" help to establish the
      speaker's attitude toward the world's evaluation of the dead poet?
   b. What is "the real thing"? Does the phrase have more than one
      meaning? What was the *underlying* cause of the poet's death?
   c. Why does the speaker say "a lot less forgotten" in line 5? How
      do these words help define his attitude toward the less forgotten?
   d. How are we to take the phrase "gone from this rotten taxable
      world to a higher standard of living"?
   e. What is the effect of such phrases as "comfy suburbs," "soupy
      summer is settling," "Sunday fathers," "all the little lawns"?
   f. Consider the effect of the rhetorical questions asked in stanza
      four. How do the machines and appliances mentioned help define
      the speaker's attitude toward his neighbors? How would you char-
      acterize his tone of voice in this stanza?

2. What change of tone do you notice in the last stanza? Point to the
   details of language that define this tone.
   a. What is the "sleep of death"?
   b. Why do "they sleep the sounder since you died"?
   c. Why is it "just as well" that now the poet "save his breath"? Is
      there a pun on "save your breath"? Explain.

Have fun with the next two poems. In "Poor Timing" notice
the use of rhyme for comic effects, *i.e.,* "clasp her in" and "as-
pirin." Is the title well chosen?

SEASIDE GOLF

John Betjeman

(1906–   )

How straight it flew, how long it flew,
  It cleared the rutty track
And, soaring, disappeared from view
  Beyond the bunker's back —
A glorious, sailing, bounding drive   5
That made me glad I was alive.

And down the fairway, far along,
  It glowed a lonely white;
I played an iron sure and strong
  And clipped it out of sight,   10
And spite of grassy banks between
I knew I'd find it on the green.

And so I did. It lay content
  Two paces from the pin;
A steady putt and then it went   15
  Oh, most securely in.
The very turf rejoiced to see
That quite unprecedented three.

Ah! seaweed smells from sandy caves
  And thyme and mist in whiffs,   20
Incoming tide, Atlantic waves
  Slapping the sunny cliffs,
Lark song and sea sounds in the air
And splendor, splendor everywhere.

Poor Timing
Phyllis McGinley

(1905–   )

I sing Saint Valentine, his day,
  I spread abroad his rumor —
A gentleman, it's safe to say,
  Who owned a sense of humor.
Most practical of jokers, he,   5
  Who bade sweethearts make merry
With flowers and birds and amorous words,
  In the month of February.
The antic, frantic,
Unromantic   10
  Middle of February.

Now, April weather's fine and fair
  For love to get a start in.
And May abets a willing pair,
  And June you lose your heart in.   15
There's many a month when wooing seems
  Both suitable and proper.
But the mating call unseasonal
  Is bound to come a cropper.

When blizzards rage with might and main   20
  And a man's best friend's his muffler,
Pity the February swain,
  That sentimental snuffler,
Whose soul must surge, whose pulse must throb
  With passionate cadenza,   25
When he yearns instead for a cozy bed
  Alone with influenza.

When winds blow up and snow comes down
  And the whole gray world seems horrider,
And every lass that sulks in town   30
  Thinks wistfully of Florider,
Pity the chapped and wintry maid
  Who'd trade the arms that clasp her in,
For Vitamin A and a nasal spray
And maybe a bottle of aspirin.   35

Who wants to bill, who cares to coo,
  Who longs for cherry-chopping,
When noses are red and fingers blue
  And the hemoglobin's dropping?
Let summer lovers droop and pine,   40
  Let springtime hearts be airy.
I wouldn't be anyone's Valentine
  In the month of February.
The spare-able terrible,
Quite unbearable   45
  Middle of February.

5

Rhythm, Sound, and Syntax

Until now we have been concerned chiefly with poetry as a *language* — with the interplay between the words and ideas and tone of a poem. We have contended that poetry and prose are not essentially different, except that the language of poetry is usually more highly organized and concentrated and intense than the language of prose, the whole poem more carefully designed to quicken the pulse and imagination, while taking hold of the mind.

We turn now to those features of poetry that distinguish it more sharply from prose, that give poetry its music and tonal color — its special power. These are the devices of sound and rhythm that are peculiar to poetry, and the special uses that poetry makes of syntax.

1. Sound

At the beginning of Chapter 1 it was noted that most poems are easily recognized by their regular pattern of end rhyming — or the repetition of the sound in the stressed syllable of the last word in the line in some regular order, such as *a b a b* or *a b b a* or *a a b b c c*, etc. (See the discussion of the sonnet's *rhyme scheme* in Chapter 3.) For practice in recognizing the rhyme scheme of a poem, pick out several poems at random and identify the sound at the end of each line by using the letters *a, b, c,* etc.

You will notice, as in the case of "The Man He Killed" (page 32), how often the rhyme scheme is ordered and regularized by separate stanzas. Can you identify the rhyme scheme of "The Man He Killed"? In the questions on this poem in Chapter 2, we might have directed attention to Hardy's skillful use of rhyme to heighten his meaning — particularly in stanza 3:

> I shot him dead because —
> Because he was my foe,
> Just so: my foe of course he was;
> That's clear enough; although

Notice that the word *although* rhymes with the word *foe*. When we consider that the idea introduced by *although* (all of stanza 4) qualifies and questions everything implied by the word *foe*, we realize that the irony is driven home dramatically by the rhyme. The very rhyme itself is ironic! Do you notice another interesting rhyme in stanza 5 of this poem? Can you explain how this rhyme contributes to the basic irony underlying the poem? Later we will see how this irony is further pointed by the syntactical arrangement of the one long sentence which comprises stanzas 3 and 4.

In addition to this easily recognizable device of *end rhyme*, the tonal color of many poems depends on slightly more subtle repetitions of sound *within* the lines of the poem. Repetition of the *initial* consonant or vowel sound of a stressed syllable in two or more closely placed words is called *alliteration*, as in "*f*ish, *f*lesh, or *f*owl," or "*red*eem" and "in*d*uce." Notice how much the humorous charm of the following poem depends on its use of rhyme and alliteration.

THE TURTLE

Ogden Nash

(1902–1971)

The turtle lives 'twixt plated decks
Which practically conceal its sex.
I think it clever of the turtle
In such a fix to be so fertile.

Repetition of the internal vowel sounds of two or more closely placed words is known as *assonance*, and repetition of an internal or end consonant sound is called *consonance*. In the following poem, line 6, "And all is *seared* with trade; *bleared, smeared* with toil" offers a good example of the former, and line 11, "And though the la*st* ligh*ts* off the black We*st* we*nt*" is a good example of the latter. Both lines also contain alliteration. See how many of these sound devices you can find in this poem.

GOD'S GRANDEUR

Gerard Manley Hopkins

(1844–1889)

The world is charged with the grandeur of God.
It will flame out, like shining from shook foil;
It gathers to a greatness, like the ooze of oil
Crushed. Why do men then now not reck his rod?
Generations have trod, have trod, have trod;   5
And all is seared with trade; bleared, smeared with toil
And wears man's smudge and shares man's smell:
    the soil
Is bare now, nor can foot feel, being shod.

And for all this, nature is never spent;
There lives the dearest freshness deep down things;   10
And though the last lights off the black West went
Oh, morning, at the brown brink eastward, springs —
Because the Holy Ghost over the bent
World broods with warm breast and with ah! bright
    wings.

Questions and Exercises

1. Which images evoke the radiance of God's world? With which others are these contrasted? How does this contrast define the theme of the poem? Is this poem as applicable to the world today as it was in the last century? Why or why not?

2. What is the rhyme scheme of this poem? Describe the structure of
   its two main divisions. What kind of poem is it?

   Skillfully used, these sound devices can charm the ear, provid-
ing a pleasure similar to that of music. They also make the poem
somehow more memorable. But it is not only for their musical
charm that these devices are used; they often contribute to the
poem's overall "meaning" by calling up an emotion closely asso-
ciated with the thing being described. As you read the following
poems, listen with your mind's ear to the effect of the sounds.
Then see if you can answer the questions following each poem.

SPRING

Gerard Manley Hopkins

(1844–1889)

Nothing is so beautiful as spring —
   When weeds, in wheels, shoot long and lovely and
         lush;
   Thrush's eggs look little low heavens, and thrush
Through the echoing timber does so rinse and wring
The ear, it strikes like lightning to hear him sing;   5
   The glassy peartree leaves and blooms, they brush
   The descending blue; that blue is all in a rush
With richness; the racing lambs too have fair their
         fling.

What is all this juice and all this joy?
   A strain of the earth's sweet being in the beginning   10
In Eden Garden. — Have, get, before it cloy,
   Before it cloud, Christ, lord, and sour with sinning,
Innocent mind and Mayday in girl and boy,
   Most, O maid's child,* thy choice and worthy the
         winning.   14

14. **maid's child:** Christ.

Questions and Exercises

1. Select several lines from "Spring" (like lines 5–8) in which the sound devices seem to you particularly effective and explain how the sounds reinforce the sense of the lines.
2. What is the rhyme scheme of "Spring"? What kind of poem is it? Describe the relationship between the first eight lines and the last six.
3. To what two things is the spring compared to in lines 9–14? Why?

No Longer Mourn for Me

William Shakespeare

(1564–1616)

No longer mourn for me when I am dead
Than you shall hear the surly, sullen bell
Give warning to the world that I am fled
From this vile world, with vilest worms to dwell.
Nay, if you read this line, remember not   5
The hand that writ it; for I love you so
That I in your sweet thoughts would be forgot
If thinking on me then should make you woe.
Oh, if, I say, you look upon this verse
When I perhaps compounded am with clay,   10
Do not so much as my poor name rehearse,
But let your love even with my life decay,
    Lest the wise world should look into your moan
    And mock you with me after I am gone.

Questions and Exercises

1. How does the rhyme scheme of this sonnet by Shakespeare differ from that of "Spring"?
2. Describe the sound effects in the first quatrain. Explain how they contribute to the emotion expressed by the speaker in these lines.
3. What is the paradox expressed in the first twelve lines? How is this paradox resolved in the last two lines of the poem? Can you explain why Shakespeare concluded with two consecutive rhyming lines (*a couplet*)?

These same sound devices often play an important role in establishing the *tone* of a poem or in dramatizing a shift in the tone of voice of the speaker. In "To An American Poet Just Dead" (page 87), there is a marked shift in the speaker's tone of voice from stanza 4 to stanza 5. Stanza 4 has a soft musical ring, somehow emphasizing the irony of the mute appliances which will not join in the traditional musical farewell to their beloved master. This musical ring is established by the alliteration of "weep wide," "melt and mourn," and "Studebakers shred . . . sound" and the assonance of "their chaplet tears" and "their gears." Notice also that the whole stanza consists of four ironic *questions*.

Stanza 5 puts a quick end to the mocking tone, and the speaker's voice suddenly becomes deadly serious with the quick, short, deadly serious answer "They won't," the seriousness emphasized by the hard sound of the "t" in "won't." This seriousness continues with the alliteration of "*s*ummer *s*unk and *s*tupefied" and the assonance of "deepen in their sleep of death," before the final return to irony in the last two lines.

2. Rhythm and Meter

This deliberate and highly specialized use of sound to convey or reinforce meaning is one of the distinguishing qualities of poetry and one of the most important resources the skillful poet has to draw on. Sound, however, is seldom found operating apart from another basic characteristic of poetry — *rhythm*, and the poetic ordering of rhythm, which is known as *meter*. It is the highly controlled blending of sound and rhythm that, more than anything else, sets poetry off from prose. And it is only when we see these two elements working together that we can appreciate the full effectiveness of each.

Most uses of the English language are to some extent rhythmical, that is, characterized by an alteration of stressed and unstressed syllables, depending on how the words are pronounced and on which words in the sentence receive the heaviest stress or emphasis. That is, in words of more than one syllable one of the syllables is more heavily accented or stressed than the other syllables — for example, *bicycle*. Similarly, in an English sentence some word or words are more heavily stressed than others;

something in the syntax of the sentence demands that this be so. Thus if I say "The boy threw the ball over the fence," *ball* and *fence* are more heavily stressed than the other words in the sentence, just as in the word *over* the "o" is more heavily stressed than "-ver." Actually, the degree of stress received by the different words and syllables of words in a sentence is relative; the sharp ear can hear four different degrees of stress on the words and syllables of the sentence as a whole. In the preceding sentence, for example, *boy* receives less stress than *ball* or *fence* but considerably more than the two *the*'s and a little more than *threw*, and about the same as the "o" in *over*. But if we were to pretend that this sentence were a line of poetry and that we were listening for only two degrees of stress, we would mark the sentence as follows: *The boy threw the ball over the fence* — and say that *boy, threw, ball*, "*o*", and *fence* were stressed and the other words and syllables unstressed. Notice that there is no regular pattern of occurrence of stressed and unstressed words or syllables. If we were to find a *regular* pattern in the occurrence of stressed and unstressed words and syllables in such a random sentence, it would be entirely accidental. Thus if someone were to say or write offhand *The boy appeared to jump before he ran*, he would have written a sentence in which every other syllable is stressed in a perfectly regular manner. (The boy appeared to jump before he ran.) The sentence has a *regular* rhythm or beat.

What the poet does is to choose and arrange the words in each *line* of his poem (the *lines* of a poem should not be confused with the sentences of a poem) so carefully that he superimposes on the line the meter or beat *that he wants it to have*, and usually he will superimpose on each line of the poem more or less the same beat. It is necessary to say "more or less" because, as we shall see, once a poet has established the beat he wants his poem to have, he achieves his most telling effects in certain lines by departing, however slightly, from the established pattern.

The meter or beat found in the random sentence above is called *iambic*, which means the regular occurrence of an unstressed syllable followed by a stressed syllable. Each *combination* of a stressed syllable with one or more unstressed syllables is called a foot in poetry. Thus if we divide the line into feet as follows, *The boy | appeared | to jump | before | he ran*, there would be five feet, each comprised of an unstressed, followed by a stressed, syllable. Such a meter is called *iambic pentameter*, the "penta" in *pentameter* being the Greek prefix for five, "meter" meaning "measure." Thus the line moves to a five-foot measure.

Iambic pentameter is the meter most frequently found in English poetry, chiefly because English speech tends to be iambic anyway. But iambic pentameter has been given authority and distinction by the fact that it was the meter in which Shakespeare composed all his plays and sonnets. In fact, the sonnet, whether Shakespearean or Italian, is always in iambic pentameter — as this line illustrates:

No long | er mourn | for me | when I | am dead

And so with the remainder of the sonnet.

English poetry makes use of only *four* kinds of metrical feet, and they are very easily recognized and remembered. They are

1) the *iamb* or *iambic* foot. Rendered: ‿ ′
2) the *trochee* or *trochaic* foot (the reverse of the iamb). Rendered: ′ ‿
3) the *anapest* or *anapestic* foot. Rendered: ‿ ‿ ′
4) the *dactyl* or *dactylic* foot (the reverse of the anapest). Rendered: ′ ‿ ‿

If two heavily stressed syllables fall together and seem to form a foot by themselves, we call this a *spondee* or *spondaic* foot; and if two unaccented syllables in a row seem to form a foot, we call this a *pyrrhic* foot.

We designate the number of feet in a line with the following Greek words:

> *di*meter — two feet
> *tri*meter — three feet
> *tetra*meter — four feet
> *penta*meter — five feet
> *hexa*meter — six feet

Very few English poems have lines with fewer than two feet or more than six. To scan a poem (or describe a poem's *scansion*) means simply to divide the lines of the poem into their metrical feet, noting the kind of foot being used and the number of feet there are per line.

Exercises

1. Choose any five poems with differing meters in the book. Copy out at least two stanzas from each poem and scan them.

2. Compare your scansion of a given poem with someone else's. Are there differences? Is one interpretation better than another? Why?

3. The Uses of Meter and Sound

To be able to scan a poem, however, and even to recognize the departures from the established meter in individual lines, is of little use to anyone unless he can tell *why* the poet is using a particular meter or a departure from the meter and *how* the poet has combined meter with sound to achieve a particular effect. To illustrate how meter and sound can be harnessed together to draw out sense, let us consider a two-line poem by Robert Frost, "The Span of Life."

> The old dog barks backward without getting up.
> I can remember when he was a pup.

This poem, whose purpose is simply to contrast the tiredness and laziness of an old dog with its liveliness as a young pup, *scans* as follows:

> The old / dog barks back / ward without / getting up.
> I can / remem / ber when he / was a pup.

Although the two lines can be divided into feet in a number of different ways, clearly the dominant type of foot is *anapestic* (‿ ‿ ′), normally a fast-moving meter. But the poet has carefully arranged the syllables in the first line in such a way as to slow the line down considerably. Notice that the second foot departs from the anapestic beat and runs together three heavy stresses, a foot we would probably have to call a triple spondee. Together with the stress on "old" in the first foot, we thus have four accented syllables jammed together in a row, the effect of which is to slow down the line and "enact" in sound the sense of difficulty with which the old dog barks backward. In addition, each of these accented syllables begins and ends with a hard consonant, making them difficult to pronounce and causing us to pause after each word and make a special effort with the mouth to say the next word. Thus the laboring line exactly corresponds with and helps us to feel the effort it costs the old dog to perform this simple action. The second line, however, with its almost completely regular series of anapests, has a quick, tripping rhythm which accords with the friskiness of the pup. The pup's nimbleness is further evoked by the smooth rapidity with which the words "can remember when" can be spoken and by the sharpness with which the word *pup* (with its two hard consonants) ends the line.

The word *bark* in the first line is what is called an *onomatopoetic* word, which means that it actually sounds like the action it describes. This word is echoed and thus reinforced by the "back" of "backward," and thus the visual image is reinforced by the sound of the line.

Read the following poem several times carefully, and scan it before answering the questions which follow.

SOUND AND SENSE*

Alexander Pope

(1688–1744)

True ease in writing comes from art, not chance,
As those move easiest who have learned to dance.
'Tis not enough no harshness gives offense,
The sound must seem an echo to the sense:
Soft is the strain when Zephyr gently blows,   5
And the smooth stream in smoother numbers flows;
But when loud surges lash the sounding shore,
The hoarse, rough verse should like the torrent roar;
When Ajax strives some rock's vast weight to throw,
The line too labors, and the words move slow;   10
Not so, when swift Camilla scours the plain,
Flies o'er the unbending corn, and skims along the
        main.
Hear how Timotheus' varied lays surprise,
And bid alternate passions fall and rise!

* From *An Essay on Criticism.*

Questions and Exercises

1. Lines 3, 4, and 14 (if *alternate* is pronounced with a stress on *ter,* as it was in eighteenth-century England) are the only completely regular lines in the poem. What is their meter? (This meter, then, is the one used to describe the meter of the whole poem. The other lines are merely variations, some great, some slight, from this basic metrical pattern.)

2. What sound effects do you find in lines 5 and 6 to reinforce the sense?

3. Lines 7 and 8 are in sharp contrast to lines 5 and 6, both in content and in the combination of sound and beat that supports this content. Can you describe this combination?

4. The effect of the sound-meter combination in line 9 is described in line 10. The line scans as follows:

When Á / jāx stríves / sŏme róck's / vàst wéight / tŏ thrów.

Explain how sound and meter, apparently at odds in the third and fourth feet, actually work together to echo the sense of the action described.

5. Analyze line 12 for its combination of sound, meter, and sense.

Study the following three poems (or excerpts) and scan them before attempting to answer the questions which follow.

ON A HUGE HILL*
John Donne
(1572–1631)

On a huge hill
Cragged and steep, Truth stands, and he that will
Reach her, about must, and about must go;
And what the hill's suddenness resists, win so;
Yet strive so, that before age, death's twilight,
Thy soul rest, for none can work in that night.

* From *Satyres III.*

Questions

1. How does the meter in lines 2, 4, and 5 and the repetitions in line 3 reinforce the sense of slow, plodding effort?

2. Line 6 is an echo of the biblical phrase "For the night cometh when no man can work." How has Donne recast this idea so as to emphasize the deliberate laboriousness involved?

FROM ULYSSES*
Alfred, Lord Tennyson
(1809–1892)

The lights begin to twinkle from the rocks;
The long day wanes; the slow moon climbs; the deep
Moans round with many voices.

* The complete poem appears on pages 112–114.

Questions

1. How do the sounds of the first line suggest the twinkling of lights off the rocks?

2. How do the sounds and the meter in the second line help to increase our sense of the slow waning of the day and the slow rising of the moon?

3. In the context of the whole poem (see page 112), does "the long day wanes" carry any connotations beyond the literal sense of the line?

Turn back to Browning's "Meeting at Night" (page 53), and analyze the way sound and meter contribute to the meaning of the poem.

REQUIEM
Robert Louis Stevenson
(1850–1894)

Under the wide and starry sky,
Dig the grave and let me lie.
Glad did I live and gladly die,
    And I laid me down with a will.

This be the verse you grave for me: 5
Here he lies where he longed to be,
Home is the sailor, home from sea,
And the hunter home from the hill.

Questions and Exercises

1. What change in the meter do you find in the last line of both stanzas? Explain the effect of this change, particularly in the second stanza.

2. What is the rhyme scheme of the whole poem? What other devices of sound has Stevenson combined with his metrical pattern to reinforce the sense of the poem?

3. There are no unusual words and almost no concrete images in this poem, yet it has had a long and continued appeal. Comment on the quality of Stevenson's diction.

Read Gwendolyn Brooks's "We Real Cool" (page 47) aloud several times and try to catch its rhythm. How would you describe this rhythm? (Notice that *all* the words are stressed.) The rhythm is created by the pause after each period and by the slight pause at the end of each line. Does this rhythm match the content of the poem? Help to establish the tone? Explain.

How does the rhythm match the language and even the grammar of this poem?

4. Poetry and Syntax

Our study has shown that the final effect of a poem upon the ear, the emotions, and the mind of a reader depends upon a subtle and complex interweaving of many verbal elements and that when words are put together in certain ways they create sounds and rhythms that are as much a part of the poem's "meaning" as the images, attitudes, and ideas the words evoke. When words are combined into the sentences of a poem (these are not necessarily the same as the *lines* of a poem, remember), however, they must be combined in accordance with certain grammatical or syntactical principles; and here again, in the very structure of his sentences, the arrangement of clauses and phrases, and in the grammatical forms he uses, the poet has further opportunity to create effects that contribute to the poem's final meaning.

In Richard Wilbur's poem "To an American Poet Just Dead" (page 87) we saw that the short, two-word sentence ("They won't.") with which the final stanza begins produced an effect of finality and deadly seriousness after the playful mockery of the preceding stanza. Short sentences obviously have a different effect upon the ear and mind from long sentences, and long sentences themselves can have many different kinds of effect, depending on the arrangement of the phrases and clauses within the sentence and on whether the verb or the whole predication comes near the beginning of the sentence or is delayed until near the end.

Here is a poem consisting of one long sentence. Let us see how the structure of this sentence affects the tone and therefore the meaning of the poem.

When I Heard The Learn'd Astronomer

Walt Whitman

(1819–1892)

When I heard the learn'd astronomer,
When the proofs, the figures, were ranged in columns
    before me,
When I was shown the charts and diagrams, to add,
    divide, and measure them,
When I sitting heard the astronomer where he
    lectured with much applause in the lecture room,
How soon unaccountable I became tired and sick,   5
Till rising and gliding out I wandered off by myself,
In the mystical moist night air, and from time to time,
Looked up in perfect silence at the stars.

The poem's first four lines consist of four subordinate "when" clauses before we come to the predication in line 5 ("I became tired and sick"). Notice also that each succeeding clause is slightly longer and grammatically more complicated than the preceding one. The effect of this repetition of *when's*, together with the increasing length and complexity of the clauses is to produce a sense of mounting boredom and exasperation with the pedantic explanations and paraphernalia of the astronomy professor. These clauses actually suggest a kind of hothouse, academic, atmosphere, even before we know what kind of statement (in the main clause) they are all leading up to.

The whole poem turns on the contrast between what comes before the main predication and what comes after it, in the final subordinate clause beginning with "Till." The speaker is, in effect, asserting that the beauty and mystery of the stars is something that must be *experienced* "in perfect silence" and that this experience "in the mystical moist night air" gives one a kind of knowledge that makes the professor's scientific abstractions seem like ignorance.

Notice finally that in this poem syntax, meter, and sound all work together toward the same end.

Questions

1. The first four lines have no definite metrical pattern. Line 5 begins to build toward a meter that becomes completely regular in the last line. What is this meter? What is the effect of this build-up and the achieving of perfect regularity in the last line?

2. What sound effects do you find in the last three lines that help to echo their sense?

Refer again to Hardy's "The Man He Killed" (page 32), and answer the following questions.

1. In what way is the third stanza syntactically different from every other stanza in the poem?

2. What is the effect of *ending* this stanza with a subordinating conjunction? (The whole fourth stanza *is* the subordinate clause introduced by the conjunction "although.")

3. How have rhyme and grammar worked together to make "although" the pivotal and crucial word in the poem?

Shelley's "Ozymandias" is a meditation suggested by the ruins of a statue of the Egyptian Pharaoh Rameses II, later found at

Thebes. The poem is often misread because its syntax is misunderstood. See if you can read it correctly.

OZYMANDIAS

Percy Bysshe Shelley

(1792–1822)

I met a traveler from an antique land
Who said: Two vast and trunkless legs of stone
Stand in the desert. Near them, on the sand,
Half sunk, a shattered visage lies, whose frown,
And wrinkled lip, and sneer of cold command,   5
Tell that its sculptor well those passions read
Which yet survive, stamped on these lifeless things,
The hand that mocked them and the heart that fed:
And on the pedestal these words appear:
"My name is Ozymandias, king of kings: 10
Look on my works, ye Mighty, and despair!"
Nothing beside remains. Round the decay
Of that colossal wreck, boundless and bare
The lone and level sands stretch far away.

Questions and Exercises

1. The grammatical problem lies in the verb *survive*. Is this a transitive or intransitive verb? If it is transitive, what are its direct objects?

2. Make a grammatical analysis of the entire sentence beginning at line 3 ("Near them") and ending at line 8 ("fed"). What is the function of *passions* in the sentence? What is the subject of *survive?*

3. Whose is "the hand that mocked"? Mocked what? Mocked how? Whose is "the heart that fed"? Fed how?

4. What ambiguity or ironic double meaning is there in the inscription on the pedestal?

5. What is the effect of the short sentence with which line 12 begins?

6. What sound and metrical devices intensify the effect of the last two lines?

Eight O'Clock

A. E. Housman

(1859–1936)

He stood, and heard the steeple
  Sprinkle the quarters on the morning town.
One, two, three, four, to market place and people
  It tossed them down.

Strapped, noosed, nighing his hour,   5
  He stood and counted them and cursed his luck.
And then the clock collected in the tower
  Its strength, and struck.

Questions

1. How effective are the meter and the sound devices of this poem as accompaniments to the dramatic action?

2. Notice the peculiar syntax of the last two lines, particularly the placing of *strength* after the prepositional phrase "in the tower." Why did Housman withhold the words *strength* and *struck* until the final line? What makes that line dramatically effective?

Reread Gwendolyn Brooks's poem "Negro Hero" (page 74), and answer the following questions.

1. Study lines 18 and 19:

> *And my first swallow of the liquor of battle bleeding black air*
>   *dying and demon noise*
> *Made me wild.*

  Can you explain the grammar of "battle bleeding black air dying and demon noise"? Can this line be read in more than one way if the grammar is interpreted differently?

2. In this line what sound effects intensify our sense of the action described and the emotions expressed?

3. Comment on the way in which the poet has used meter to control the tone and dramatize the meaning of lines 33 through 37 ("In a Southern city — black man's blood").

WHAT IF A MUCH OF A WHICH OF A WIND

E. E. Cummings

(1894–1962)

what if a much of a which of a wind
gives the truth to summer's lie;
bloodies with dizzying leaves the sun
and yanks immortal stars awry?
Blow king to beggar and queen to seem   5
(blow friend to fiend:blow space to time)
—when skies are hanged and oceans drowned,
the single secret will still be man

what if a keen of a lean wind flays
screaming hills with sleet and snow: 10
strangles valleys by ropes of thing
and stifles forests in white ago?
Blow hope to terror;blow seeing to blind
(blow pity to envy and soul to mind)
—whose hearts are mountains, roots are trees,   15
it's they shall cry hello to the spring

what if a dawn of a doom of a dream
bites this universe in two,
peels forever out of his grave
and sprinkles nowhere with me and you?   20
Blow soon to never and never to twice
(blow life to isn't:blow death to was)
—all nothing's only our hugest home;
the most who die,the more we live

Questions and Exercises

1. Explain how and why Cummings uses certain words as unexpected
   parts of speech.

2. What is the poem's theme? How is it embodied by the different images in each stanza? Are the syntactical experiments essential to the success of the image? to the creation of sound effects which underscore the sense of the poem?

3. Discuss, in terms of this poem, Archibald MacLeish's statement (page 22), that "a poem must not mean but be."

6

Poems for Pleasure

Everything we have said so far implies that poetry must be *experienced* — that is, *heard* and *felt,* as well as understood — in order to be fully appreciated. It should also be enjoyed. Poetry brings a pleasure that can be learned — with practice and concentration, and with a willingness to "give" yourself to the poem.

The poems in this section are offered, without comment or question, for your pleasure. Your pleasure, however, will be greatly enhanced if you approach them with all the understanding you now possess — of the role of subject, theme, imagery, speaker, sound, and grammar — and with the sixth sense that comes to those who have given themselves actively to many poems.

The Human Heart in Conflict

THE BOARDER

Louis Simpson

(1923-   )

The time is after dinner. Cigarettes
  Glow on the lawn;
Glasses begin to tinkle; TV sets
  Have been turned on.

The moon is brimming like a glass of beer   5
   Above the town,
And love keeps her appointments — "Harry's here!"
   "I'll be right down."

But the pale stranger in the furnished room
   Lies on his back   10
Looking at paper roses, how they bloom.
   And ceilings crack.

MINIVER CHEEVY

Edwin Arlington Robinson

(1869–1935)

Miniver Cheevy, child of scorn,
   Grew lean while he assailed the seasons;
He wept that he was ever born,
   And he had reasons.

Miniver loved the days of old   5
   When swords were bright and steeds were prancing;
The vision of a warrior bold
   Would set him dancing.

Miniver sighed for what was not,
   And dreamed, and rested from his labors;   10
He dreamed of Thebes and Camelot,
   And Priam's neighbors.

Miniver mourned the ripe renown
   That made so many a name so fragrant;
He mourned Romance, now on the town,   15
   And Art, a vagrant.

Miniver loved the Medici,
   Albeit he had never seen one;
He would have sinned incessantly
   Could he have been one.   20

Miniver cursed the commonplace
   And eyed a khaki suit with loathing;
He missed the medieval grace
   Of iron clothing.

Miniver scorned the gold he sought,   25
   But sore annoyed was he without it;
Miniver thought, and thought, and thought,
   And thought about it.

Miniver Cheevy, born too late,
   Scratched his head and kept on thinking;   30
Miniver coughed, and called it fate,
   And kept on drinking.

ULYSSES

Alfred, Lord Tennyson

(1809–1892)

It little profits that an idle king,
By this still hearth, among these barren crags,
Matched with an aged wife, I mete and dole*
Unequal laws unto a savage race,*
That hoard, and sleep, and feed, and know not me.   5
I cannot rest from travel; I will drink
Life to the lees. All times I have enjoyed

---

3. *mete and dole:* measure out and give.   4. ***Unequal laws . . . savage race:***
i.e., because unable to force his subjects to conform to any standard
code of laws.

Greatly, have suffered greatly, both with those
That loved me, and alone; on shore, and when
Through scudding drifts the rainy Hyades*   10
Vexed the dim sea. I am become a name;
For always roaming with a hungry heart
Much have I seen and known — cities of men
And manners, climates, councils, governments,
Myself not least, but honored of them all —   15
And drunk delight of battle with my peers,
Far on the ringing plains of windy Ṭroy.
I am a part of all that I have met;
Yet all experience is an arch wherethrough
Gleams that untraveled world whose margin fades   20
Forever and forever when I move.
How dull it is to pause, to make an end,
To rust unburnished, not to shine in use!
As though to breathe were life. Life piled on life
Were all too little, and of one to me   25
Little remains; but every hour is saved
From that eternal silence, something more,
A bringer of new things; and vile it were
For some three suns to store and hoard myself,
And this gray spirit yearning in desire   30
To follow knowledge like a sinking star,
Beyond the utmost bound of human thought.

    This is my son, mine own Telemachus,
To whom I leave the scepter and the isle* —
Well-loved of me, discerning to fulfill   35
This labor, by slow prudence to make mild
A rugged people, and through soft degrees
Subdue them to the useful and the good.
Most blameless is he, centered in the sphere
Of common duties, decent not to fail   40

10. **Hyades:** constellation associated with the spring rains.   34. *isle:*
Ithaca, Ulysses' kingdom.

In offices of tenderness, and pay
Meet* adoration to my household gods,
When I am gone. He works his work, I mine.

   There lies the port; the vessel puffs her sail;
There gloom the dark, broad seas. My mariners,   45
Souls that have toiled, and wrought, and thought with
     me —
That ever with a frolic welcome took
The thunder and the sunshine, and opposed*
Free hearts, free foreheads — you and I are old;
Old age hath yet his honor and his toil;   50
Death closes all; but something ere the end,
Some work of noble note, may yet be done,
Not unbecoming men that strove with gods.
The lights begin to twinkle from the rocks;
The long day wanes; the slow moon climbs; the deep   55
Moans round with many voices. Come, my friends.
'Tis not too late to seek a newer world.
Push off, and sitting well in order smite
The sounding furrows; for my purpose holds
To sail beyond the sunset, and the baths   60
Of all the western stars, until I die.
It may be that the gulfs will wash us down;
It may be we shall touch the Happy Isles,*
And see the great Achilles,* whom we knew.
Though much is taken, much abides; and though   65
We are not now that strength which in old days
Moved earth and heaven, that which we are, we are —
One equal temper of heroic hearts,
Made weak by time and fate, but strong in will
To strive, to seek, to find, and not to yield.   70

---

42. *Meet:* fitting.   48. *opposed:* met all events with.   63. *Happy Isles:*
home of warrior heroes after death.   64. *Achilles:* mightiest of the
Greek warriors who fought at Troy.

THE PARABLE OF THE OLD MAN AND THE YOUNG

Wilfred Owen

(1893–1918)

So Abram rose, and clave the wood, and went,
And took the fire with him, and a knife.
And as they sojourned both of them together,
Isaac the firstborn spake and said, My Father,
Behold the preparations, fire and iron,   5
But where the lamb for this burnt offering?
Then Abram bound the youth with belts and straps,
And builded parapets and trenches there,
And stretchèd forth the knife to slay his son.
When lo! an angel called him out of heaven,   10
Saying, Lay not thy hand upon the lad,
Neither do anything to him. Behold,
A ram, caught in a thicket by its horns;
Offer the Ram of Pride instead of him.
But the old man would not so, but slew his son,   15
And half the seed of Europe, one by one.

PORTRAIT OF THE ARTIST AS A PREMATURELY OLD MAN

Ogden Nash

(1902–1971)

It is common knowledge to every schoolboy and
     even every Bachelor of Arts,
That all sin is divided into two parts.
One kind of sin is called a sin of commission, and
     that is very important,   5
And it is what you are doing when you are doing
     something you ortant,

And the other kind of sin is just the opposite and is
    called a sin of omission and is equally bad in
    the eyes of all right-thinking people, from Billy   ¹⁰
    Sunday to Buddha,
And it consists of nòt having done something you
    shuddha.
I might as well give you my opinion of these two
    kinds of sin as long as, in a way, against each   ¹⁵
    other we are pitting them,
And that is, don't bother your head about sins of
    commission because however sinful, they
    must at least be fun or else you wouldn't be
    committing them.   ²⁰
It is the sin of omission, the second kind of sin,
That lays eggs under your skin.
The way you get really painfully bitten
Is by the insurance you haven't taken out and the
    checks you haven't added up the stubs of and   ²⁵
    the appointments you haven't kept and the
    bills you haven't paid and the letters you
    haven't written.
Also, about sins of omission there is one particu-
    larly painful lack of beauty,   ³⁰
Namely, it isn't as though it had been a riotous red-
    letter day or night every time you neglected to
    do your duty;
You didn't get a wicked forbidden thrill
Every time you let a policy lapse or forgot to pay   ³⁵
    a bill;
You didn't slap the lads in the tavern on the back
    and loudly cry Whee,
Let's all fail to write just one more letter before we
    go home, and this round of unwritten letters   ⁴⁰
    is on me.
No, you never get any fun
Out of the things you haven't done,
But they are the things that I do not like to be amid,

Because the suitable things you didn't do give you   45
    a lot more trouble than the unsuitable things
    you did.
The moral is that it is probably better not to sin at
    all, but if some kind of sin you must be pur-
    suing,   50
Well, remember to do it by doing rather than by
    not doing.

The Human Comedy

THE FATHER

John Holmes

(1904–1962)

Hearing his son and daughter
Laugh, and talk of dances, theaters,
Of their school, and friends,
And books,
Taking it all for granted, —   5
He sighs a bit,
Remembering wistfully
A certain mill town
And his boyhood there,
And puts his arm   10
Across his son's broad shoulder,
Dumbly, as fathers do.

CONVERSATION WITH GRANDFATHER

Charles Arnhold

(1945–   )

"The only village band I ever heard,"
    I said, "was under square-clipped linden trees

In Sirmione,* playing barcarolles,
  That woman's fickle — such light pleasantries."
"*Our* band," Grandfather said, "was strong on brass,   5
  It did 'The Stars and Stripes Forever' best;
(Us kids burned punk; mosquitoes don't like punk.)
  They encored with 'Juanita' by request."

"I couldn't go barefoot in Singapore,
  The little cobras hid in the long grass,"   10
I told him. He said, "That's too bad, a boy
  Has such short barefoot time, the hot days pass —
And then he's shoed for good and all! I used
  To pick wild-flowers with my toes, which got
Quite brown in summer, lost their pinched-in look.   15
  You know a lot and you *don't* know a lot."

"You never ate an apple that was green
  And hooked right from the tree. Now, that's a shame!
An apple that is ripe and yours by rights
  Is bound to taste a little flat and tame.   20
Oh, sure — you've eaten caviar, sea-slug,
  Haggis and bouillabaise, Strasburg paté —
But never clams and corn, steamed on the beach —
  They taste inferior, any other way."

He claims, "The prettiest gals in all the world   25
  Are small-town Kansas gals. What do you say?"
"They're pretty," I admit, "but the Hong Kong
  Eurasian girls are prettier." This way
We try communication when we meet,
  With firm good will. His eyes and mouth are mine,   30
And there's no malice in us, but our thoughts
  Run parallel, each on a different line!

3. *Sirmione:* town in northern Italy.

My Last Duchess

Robert Browning

(1812–1889)

That's my last Duchess painted on the wall,
Looking as if she were alive. I call
That piece a wonder, now: Fra Pandolf's hands
Worked busily a day, and there she stands.
Will't please you sit and look at her? I said   5
"Fra Pandolf" by design, for never read
Strangers like you that pictured countenance,
The depth and passion of its earnest glance,
But to myself they turned (since none puts by
The curtain I have drawn for you, but I)   10
And seemed as they would ask me, if they durst,
How such a glance came there; so, not the first
Are you to turn and ask thus. Sir, 'twas not
Her husband's presence only, called that spot
Of joy into the Duchess' cheek: perhaps   15
Fra Pandolf chanced to say, "Her mantle laps
Over my lady's wrist too much," or "Paint
Must never hope to reproduce the faint
Half-flush that dies along her throat"; such stuff
Was courtesy, she thought, and cause enough   20
For calling up that spot of joy. She had
A heart — how shall I say? — too soon made glad,
Too easily impressed; she liked whate'er
She looked on, and her looks went everywhere.
Sir, 'twas all one! My favor at her breast,   25
The dropping of the daylight in the west,
The bough of cherries some officious fool
Broke in the orchard for her, the white mule
She rode with round the terrace — all and each
Would draw from her alike the approving speech,   30
Or blush, at least. She thanked men — good! but
    thanked

Somehow — I know not how — as if she ranked
My gift of a nine-hundred-years-old name
With anybody's gift. Who'd stoop to blame
This sort of trifling? Even had you skill   35
In speech — (which I have not) — to make your will
Quite clear to such an one, and say, "Just this
Or that in you disgusts me; here you miss,
Or there exceed the mark" — and if she let
Herself be lessoned so, nor plainly set   40
Her wits to yours, forsooth, and made excuse,
— E'en then would be some stooping; and I choose
Never to stoop. Oh sir, she smiled, no doubt,
Whene'er I passed her; but who passed without
Much the same smile? This grew; I gave commands;   45
Then all smiles stopped together. There she stands
As if alive. Will't please you rise? We'll meet
The company below, then. I repeat,
The Count your master's known munificence
Is ample warrant that no just pretence*   50
Of mine for dowry will be disallowed;
Though his fair daughter's self, as I avowed
At starting, is my object. Nay, we'll go
Together down, sir. Notice Neptune, though,
Taming a sea horse, thought a rarity,   55
Which Claus of Innsbruck cast in bronze for me!

50. *pretence:* claim.

SONG

John Donne

(1572–1631)

Go and catch a falling star,
  Get with child a mandrake root,*
Tell me where all past years are,
  Or who cleft the Devil's foot;

2. *mandrake root:* the mandragora, believed to have supernatural powers.

Teach me to hear mermaids singing,   5
Or to keep off envy's stinging,
    And find
    What wind
Serves to advance an honest mind.

If thou be'st born to strange sights,   10
    Things invisible go see,
Ride ten thousand days and nights
    Till age snow white hairs on thee;
Thou, when thou return'st, wilt tell me
All strange wonders that befell thee,   15
    And swear
    No where
Lives a woman true and fair.

If thou find'st one let me know,   20
    Such a pilgrimage were sweet;
Yet do not, I would not go,
    Though at next door we might meet;
Though she were true when you met her,
And last till you write your letter,   25
    Yet she
    Will be
False, ere I come, to two or three.

SONNET CXXX

William Shakespeare

(1564–1616)

My mistress' eyes are nothing like the sun;
Coral is far more red than her lips' red;
If snow be white, why then her breasts are dun;
If hairs be wires, black wires grow on her head.
I have seen roses damasked, red and white,   5

But no such roses see I in her cheeks;
And in some perfumes is there more delight
Than in the breath that from my mistress reeks.
I love to hear her speak, yet well I know
That music hath a far more pleasing sound;   10
I grant I never saw a goddess go;
My mistress, when she walks, treads on the ground.
   And yet, by heaven, I think my love as rare
   As any she belied with false compare.

THE LATEST DECALOGUE*

Arthur Hugh Clough

(1819–1861)

Thou shalt have one God only; who
Would be at the expense of two?
No graven images may be
Worshipped, except the currency.
Swear not at all; for, for thy curse   5
Thine enemy is none the worse.
At church on Sunday to attend
Will serve to keep the world thy friend.
Honor thy parents; that is, all
From whom advancement may befall.   10
Thou shalt not kill; but need'st not strive
Officiously to keep alive.
Do not adultery commit;
Advantage rarely comes of it.
Thou shalt not steal: an empty feat,   15
When it's so lucrative to cheat.
Bear not false witness; let the lie
Have time on its own wings to fly.
Thou shalt not covet, but tradition
Approves all forms of competition.   20

Decalogue: name for the Ten Commandments.

SILENCE

Marianne Moore

(1887–1972)

My father used to say,
"Superior people never make long visits,
have to be shown Longfellow's grave
or the glass flowers at Harvard.
Self-reliant like the cat —   5
that takes its prey to privacy,
the mouse's limp tail hanging like a shoelace from its
    mouth —
they sometimes enjoy solitude,
and can be robbed of speech
by speech which has delighted them.   10
The deepest feeling always shows itself in silence;
not in silence, but restraint."
Nor was he insincere in saying, "Make my house your inn."
Inns are not residences.

Man and Nature

IT IS A BEAUTEOUS EVENING, CALM AND FREE

William Wordsworth

(1770–1850)

It is a beauteous evening, calm and free,
The holy time is quiet as a nun
Breathless with adoration; the broad sun
Is sinking down in its tranquility;
The gentleness of heaven broods o'er the sea: 5
Listen! the mighty Being is awake,
And doth with his eternal motion make

A sound like thunder — everlastingly.
Dear child! dear girl! that walkest with me here,
If thou appear untouched by solemn thought,   10
Thy nature is not therefore less divine:
Thou liest in Abraham's bosom all the year;
And worship'st at the Temple's inner shrine,
God being with thee when we know it not.

SPRING AND ALL

Part I

William Carlos Williams

(1883–1963)

By the road to the contagious hospital
under the surge of the blue
mottled clouds driven from the
northeast — a cold wind. Beyond, the
waste of broad, muddy fields   5
brown with dried weeds, standing and fallen

patches of standing water
the scattering of tall trees

All along the road the reddish
purplish, forked, upstanding, twiggy   10
stuff of bushes and small trees
with dead, brown leaves under them
leafless vines —

Lifeless in appearance, sluggish
dazed spring approaches —   15

They enter the new world naked,
cold, uncertain of all

save that they enter. All about them
the cold, familiar wind —

Now the grass, tomorrow   20
the stiff curl of wildcarrot leaf
One by one objects are defined —
It quickens: clarity, outline of leaf

But now the stark dignity of
entrance — Still, the profound change   25
has come upon them: rooted, they
grip down and begin to awaken

PASTORAL

Robert Hillyer

(1895–1961)

The wise old apple tree in spring,
Though split and hollow, makes a crown
Of such fantastic blossoming
We cannot let them cut it down.
It bears no fruit, but honey bees   5
Prefer it to the other trees.

The orchard man chalks his mark
And says, "This empty shell must go."
We nod and rub it off the bark
As soon as he goes down the row.   10
Each spring he looks bewildered. "Queer,
I thought I marked this thing last year."

Ten orchard men have come and gone
Since first I saw my grandfather
Slyly erase it. I'm the one   15
To do it now. As I defer

The showy veteran's removal
My grandson nods his full approval.

Like mine, my fellow ancient's roots
Are deep in the last century   20
From which our memories send shoots
For all our grandchildren to see
How spring, inviting bloom and rhyme,
Defeats the orchard men of time.

COMPOSED UPON WESTMINSTER BRIDGE

William Wordsworth

(1770–1850)

Earth has not anything to show more fair;
Dull would he be of soul who could pass by
A sight so touching in its majesty:
This city now doth, like a garment, wear
The beauty of the morning; silent, bare,   5
Ships, towers, domes, theaters, and temples lie
Open unto the fields, and to the sky;
All bright and glittering in the smokeless air.
Never did sun more beautifully steep
In his first splendor, valley, rock, or hill;   10
Ne'er saw I, never felt, a calm so deep!
The river glideth at its own sweet will;
Dear God! the very houses seem asleep;
And all that mighty heart is lying still!

TARGET

R. P. Lister

(1914–   )

The moon holds nothing in her arms;
She is as empty as a drum.

She is a cipher, though she charms;
   She is delectable but dumb.
She has no factories or farms,   5
   Or men to sound the fire alarms
When the marauding missiles come.

We have no cause to spare that face
   Suspended fatly in the sky.
She does not help the human race.   10
   Surely, she shines when bats fly by
And burglars seek their burgling place
   And lovers in a soft embrace
Among the whispering bushes lie —

But that is all. Dogs still will bark   15
   When cottage doors are lightly knocked
And poachers crawl about the park
   Cursing the glint on guns half cocked;
None of the creatures of the dark
   Will, in their self-absorption, mark   20
That visage growing slightly pocked.

When Serpents Bargain for the Right to Squirm

E. E. Cummings

(1894–1962)

when serpents bargain for the right to squirm
and the sun strikes to gain a living wage —
when thorns regard their roses with alarm
and rainbows are insured against old age

when every thrush may sing no new moon in   5
if all screech-owls have not okayed his voice
—and any wave signs on the dotted line
or else an ocean is compelled to close

when the oak begs permission of the birch
to make an acorn—valleys accuse their   10
mountains of having altitude — and march
denounces april as a saboteur

then we'll believe in that incredible
unanimal mankind(and not until)

Man and Society

DINNER GUEST: ME

Langston Hughes

(1902–1967)

I know I am
The Negro Problem
Being wined and dined,
Answering the usual questions
That come to white mind   5
Which seeks demurely
To probe in polite way
The why and wherewithal
Of darkness U.S.A. —
Wondering how things got this way   10
In current democratic night,
Murmuring gently
Over *fraises du bois*,*
"I'm so ashamed of being white,"

The lobster is delicious,   15
The wine divine,
And center of attention
At the damask table, mine.
To be a Problem on

13. *fraises du bois:* wood strawberries.

Park Avenue at eight 20
Is not so bad.
Solutions to the Problem,
Of course, wait.

A Semi-Revolution

Robert Frost

(1874–1963)

I advocate a semi-revolution.
The trouble with a total revolution
(Ask any reputable Rosicrucian*)
Is that it brings the same class up on top.
Executives of skillful execution 5
Will therefore plan to go halfway and stop.
Yes, revolutions are the only salves,
But they're one thing that should be done by halves.

3. **Rosicrucian:** member of an organization descended from a 17th- and 18th-century mystical society.

A Total Revolution

(An Answer for Robert Frost)

Oscar Williams

(1900–1964)

I advocate a total revolution.
The trouble with a semi-revolution,
It's likely to be slow as evolution.
Who wants to spend the ages in collusion
With Compromise, Complacence, and Confusion? 5
As for the same class coming up on top
That's wholecloth from the propaganda shop;
The old saw says there's loads of room on top,

That's where the poor should really plan to stop.
And speaking of those people called the "haves,"   10
Who own the whole cow and must have the calves
(And plant the wounds so they can sell the salves)
They won't be stopped by doing things by halves.
I say that for a permanent solution
There's nothing like a total revolution!   15

P.S. And may I add by way of a conclusion
    I wouldn't dream to ask a Rosicrucian.

IN SCHRAFFT'S

W. H. Auden

(1907–   )

Having finished the Blue-plate Special
And reached the coffee stage,
Stirring her cup she sat,
A somewhat shapeless figure
Of indeterminate age   5
In an undistinguished hat.

When she lifted her eyes it was plain
That our globular furore,
Our international rout
Of sin and apparatus   10
And dying men galore,
Was not being bothered about.

Which of the seven heavens
Was responsible her smile
Wouldn't be sure but attested   15
That, whoever it was, a god
Worth kneeling-to for a while
Had tabernacled and rested.

For My People

Margaret Walker

(1915–   )

For my people everywhere singing their slave songs re-
   peatedly: their dirges and their ditties and their blues
   and jubilees, praying their prayers nightly to an un-
   known god, bending their knees humbly to an unseen
   power;

For my people lending their strength to the years: to the
   gone years and the now years and the maybe years,
   washing ironing cooking scrubbing sewing mending
   hoeing plowing digging planting pruning patching
   dragging along never gaining never reaping never
   knowing and never understanding;

For my playmates in the clay and dust and sand of Ala-
   bama backyards playing baptizing and preaching,
   and doctor and jail and soldier and school and mama
   and cooking and playhouse and concert and store and
   Miss Choomby and hair and company;

For the cramped bewildered years we went to school to
   learn to know the reasons why and the answers to
   and the people who and the places where and the
   days when, in memory of the bitter hours when we
   discovered we were black and poor and small and
   different and nobody wondered and nobody under-
   stood;

For the boys and girls who grew in spite of these things to
   be Man and Woman, to laugh and dance and sing and
   play and drink their wine and religion and success,
   to marry their playmates and bear children and then
   die of consumption and anemia and lynching;

For my people thronging 47th Street in Chicago and Lenox
   Avenue in New York and Rampart Street in New
   Orleans, lost disinherited dispossessed and HAPPY
   people filling the cabarets and taverns and other

people's pockets needing bread and shoes and milk
and land and money and Something — Something all
our own;

For my people walking blindly, spreading joy, losing time
being lazy, sleeping when hungry, shouting when
burdened, drinking when hopeless, tied and shackled
and tangled among ourselves by the unseen creatures
who tower over us omnisciently and laugh;

For my people blundering and groping and floundering in
the dark of churches and schools and clubs and so-
cieties, associations and councils and committees
and conventions, distressed and disturbed and de-
ceived and devoured by money-hungry glory-craving
leeches, preyed on by facile force of state and fad and
novelty by false prophet and holy believer;

For my people standing staring trying to fashion a better
way from confusion from hypocrisy and misunder-
standing, trying to fashion a world that will hold all
the people all the faces all the adams and eves and
their countless generations;

Let a new earth rise. Let another world be born. Let a
bloody peace be written in the sky. Let a second gen-
eration full of courage issue forth, let a people loving
freedom come to growth, let a beauty full of healing
and a strength of final clenching be the pulsing in our
spirits and our blood. Let the martial songs be writ-
ten, let the dirges disappear. Let a race of men now
rise and take control!

THE GIFT OUTRIGHT

Robert Frost

(1874–1963)

The land was ours before we were the land's.
She was our land more than a hundred years
Before we were her people. She was ours

In Massachusetts, in Virginia,
But we were England's, still colonials,   5
Possessing what we still were unpossessed by,
Possessed by what we now no more possessed.
Something we were withholding made us weak
Until we found out that it was ourselves
We were withholding from our land of living,   10
And forthwith found salvation in surrender.
Such as we were we gave ourselves outright
(The deed of gift was many deeds of war)
To the land vaguely realizing westward,
But still unstoried, artless, unenhanced,   15
Such as she was, such as she would become.

THE CITY OF YES AND THE CITY OF NO

Yevgeny Yevtushenko

(1933–   )

I am like a train
            rushing for many years now
between the city of Yes
            and the city of No.
My nerves are strained   5
            like wires
between the city of No
            and the city of Yes.

Everything is deadly,
            everyone frightened, in the city of No.   10
It's like a study furnished with dejection.
In it every object is frowning, withholding something,
and every portrait looks out suspiciously.
Every morning its parquet floors are polished with bile,
its sofas are made of falsehood, its walls of misfortune.   15
You'll get lots of good advice in it — like hell you will! —

not a bunch of flowers, or even a greeting.
Typewriters are chattering a carbon-copy answer:
"No — no — no . . . No — no — no. No — no — no."
And when the lights go out altogether,   20
the ghosts in it begin their gloomy ballet.
You'll get a ticket to leave — like hell you will! —
to leave the black town of No.

But in the town of Yes —
        life's like the song of a thrush.   25
This town's without walls —
        just like a nest.
The sky is asking you to take any star
        you like in your hand.
Lips ask for yours, without any shame,   30
softly murmuring:
        "Ah — all that nonsense!"

And in no one is there even a trace of suspicion,
and lowing herds are offering their milk,
and daisies, teasing, are asking to be picked,   35
and wherever you want to be, you are instantly there,
taking any train, or plane, or ship that you like.
And water, faintly murmuring, whispers through the
    years:
"Yes — yes — yes. Yes — yes — yes. Yes — yes — yes."
To tell the truth, the snag is it's a bit boring at times,   40
to be given so much, almost without any effort,
in that shining multicolored city of Yes.

Better let me be tossed around —
        to the end of my days,
between the city of Yes   45
        and the city of No!
Let my nerves be strained
        like wires
between the city of No
        and the city of Yes!   50

GLOSSARY OF LITERARY TERMS

abstract: that which refers to general ideas or qualities as distinct from concrete things.

accent: emphasis on one syllable, stress: ác cent.

alliteration: repetition of an initial consonant or sound: "maggie and milly and molly and may."

ambiguity: quality of having two or more possible (not necessarily incompatible) meanings. Ambiguity is often used intentionally in poetry.

anapest (anapestic): a metrical foot in which two unaccented syllables are followed by an accented one. (See *meter.*)

assonance: repetition of the stressed vowel in succeeding words, but not of the consonants: awake / fate.

ballad: a simple, narrative poem, originally intended to be sung. The story often deals with primitive deeds and emotions. The traditional ballad stanza is four lines, rhyming *abcb.*

blank verse: unrhymed verse (usually iambic lines of five feet).

concrete: something that has actual existence as opposed to abstractions; particular, real circumstances as distinct from general ideas.

connotation: the cluster of meanings associated with a word, from its sound or look or our past experience of the word — as opposed to denotation, the accepted, dictionary definition. Connotations give greater emotional value to the word, enriching it with a wide range of meanings and suggestions.

consonance: repetition of the final consonant in the stressed syllables of words though the vowels are different: born / burn; lonely / slowly.

couplet: a two-line stanza with end rhyme, the lines usually being of the same length:
> True ease in writing comes from art, not chance,
> As those move easiest who have learned to dance.

dactyl (dactylic): a kind of rhythmic foot in which an accented syllable is succeeded by two unaccented ones. (See *meter.*)

denotation: that aspect of a word's meaning which names or points to the class of objects to which it refers (its dictionary meaning).

diction: the use of words in speech or writing; good diction in poetry suggests the careful, accurate use of words for a particular meaning or emotional effect or tonal coloring.

dissonance: harsh sounds, as opposed to harmony.

elegy: a poem of lament, mourning, or deep, serious thoughts.

epic: a long, narrative poem that recounts the heroic exploits of one central, noble character (Homer's *Odyssey* tells the adventures of the hero Odysseus).

figurative language: writing in which words are used beyond their literal meaning, and particularly to suggest a picture or image; some figures of speech are simile, metaphor, symbol, personification, etc.

foot: a rhythmic subdivision of a line of poetry. The common feet in English poetry are *iambic, trochaic, anapestic,* and *dactylic.* (See *meter.*)

free verse: poetry that does not have regular form or rhythm.

haiku (hokku): a Japanese poem of three lines: the first line having five syllables, the second seven, and the third five again. The haiku creates a clear picture which arouses an emotional response and a further insight. (See pages 51–52).

iamb (iambic): a metrical foot consisting of one unaccented followed by one accented syllable:

image: a concrete description of any sense impression, as a picture is for the sense of sight.

imagery: the collection of images within a poem.

internal rhyme: rhyme occurring within a single line.

irony: a statement whose intended meaning is the opposite of its apparent meaning; not to be confused with *sarcasm,* which is always harsh and cutting.

lyric: a poem expressing a single, strong emotion, usually the personal feelings of the speaker.

metaphor: a figure of speech that indirectly compares two things that are similar in some way; an implied analogy.

meter: division of the poetic line into equal units, each unit — or foot — composed of a fixed number of stressed and unstressed syllables. There are different patterns of meter according to the way the stressed syllables are arranged in the line. (See pages 96–100.)

monologue: a lengthy speech by one person only.

mood: the feeling that pervades a poem, just as a person's mood may be thoughtful, exuberant, bitter, etc. (Compare *tone.*)

muse: Nine goddesses in Greek mythology presided over the arts and sciences. Those that helped and inspired poets were Calliope for epic poetry, Erato for lyric poetry, especially love poetry, Polyhymnia for religious poetry, and Euterpe for music.

narrative poem: a non-dramatic poem that tells a story.

octave: the first eight lines of a sonnet.

ode: a lyric poem that is serious and dignified, usually in praise of some thing or some idea.

onomatopoeia: the effect when words are made to sound like the thing they mean: the "buzz" of flies, the "whirr" of a saw.

overstatement: exaggeration.

pace (timing): See pages 99 and *ff.*

paradox: a seemingly contradictory statement.

pentameter: a line of verse that has five feet.

paraphrase: a prose restatement of the literal idea underlying a poem.

personification: a figure of speech that imagines animals, things, abstract ideas, moral qualities, etc., as persons or as having human qualities.

quatrain: a stanza consisting of four lines.

refrain: one or more lines repeated usually at the end of every stanza; sometimes the refrain is slightly varied for development or emphasis.

rhyme: the repetition of identical or similar sounds at intervals in a poem: most common is *end rhyme,* where the last words in alternate or successive lines rhyme. Other forms of rhyme are *internal rhyme, alliteration, assonance,* and *consonance.* (See pages 9 and *ff.*)

rhythm: movement that has a recurring beat, accent, measure, or cycle.

run-on line: a line of poetry whose meaning and grammatical structure do not stop at the end of the line but run over into the next line.

scan: to study the metrical pattern of verse, dividing the line into feet and meter in a mechanical way.

sestet: the last six lines of a sonnet.

simile: direct comparison of two things that are alike in some respect, usually with the words *like* or *as.*

spondaic: (spondee): a metrical foot consisting of two consecutive stressed syllables. (*See* meter.)

stanza: a regular grouping of two or more lines of a poem to form divisions; usually stanzas share the same line length, meter, and rhyme pattern. Regular stanzas are couplets (two lines), tercets, or triplets (three lines), and quatrains (four lines).

stress: emphasis on one syllable or word over another in poetry; accent. (See *meter*.)

structure: the framework of the poem, as understood through its different patterns and development.

symbol: something which stands for, or suggests, a larger and more undefinable idea.

tetrameter: a line of poetry that has four feet.

texture: different patterns of the poem that may be studied separately from its structure — such as sound texture, rhythm, metaphors, imagery, rhyme, etc.

timing: tempo as in music, relative speed or slowness of the poem; also the general movement of the poem as created by its rhythm.

tone: the attitude of the speaker toward his subject and audience in a poem; as a tone of voice may be solemn, formal, informal, ironic, sympathetic, etc.

trimeter: a line of poetry that has three feet.

triplet: a stanza of three lines, preferably called *tercet*.

verse: loosely used, any piece of poetry; more exactly, poetry considered by its rhythmical and rhyming aspects. While the word *poetry* suggests the power of feeling and thought, *verse* connotes simply the mechanical elements.

INDEX OF TITLES AND AUTHORS

NOPQRSTUVWXYZ–A–82